Between Dreaming and Recognition Seeking

The Emergence of Dialogical Self Theory

Hubert J. M. Hermans

UNIVERSITY PRESS OF AMERICA, ® INC.
Lanham • Boulder • New York • Toronto • Plymouth, UK

Copyright © 2012 by
University Press of America,® Inc.
4501 Forbes Boulevard
Suite 200
Lanham, Maryland 20706
UPA Acquisitions Department (301) 459-3366

10 Thornbury Road
Plymouth PL6 7PP
United Kingdom

Library of Congress Control Number: 2012934919
ISBN: 978-0-7618-5887-4 (paperback : alk. paper)
eISBN: 978-0-7618-5888-1

Cover image: *Invisible Sisyphus* by Hubert J. M. Hermans.

∞™The paper used in this publication meets the minimum
requirements of American National Standard for Information
Sciences—Permanence of Paper for Printed Library Materials,
ANSI Z39.48-1992

To my brothers Math, Ruud, Harry
and my aunt Mary
with whom I shared many of the
experiences presented in this book

Contents

Acknowledgments

I thank Agnieszka Hermans-Konopka for her numerous comments and suggestions during the writing of this book and for motivating me to compose the text in a personal way. I also thank Leiba Stuart-Young, for her valuable contribution with proofreading and editing the manuscript's English language.

Introduction

I wrote this book as an adventure in "invitational storytelling." I share some significant events in my personal and professional life, to which you *answer* by investigating some significant events in yours. In particular, I will focus on some personally impressive events in my life. I invite you to respond, in the present book, by writing about some personal events in your life as a fertile basis for meaning making.

I will not just tell my story "as it is," but I use a particular "instrument" that makes the stories "sound" in an unusual way. This instrument is a particular social-scientific theory that will shed an unexpected light on both my and your stories. The name of this theory is "Dialogical Self Theory" to which I devoted, together with my colleagues, the past 20 years of my life. After its initial publication in *the American Psychologist* (1992), I became more and more involved in the further development of this theory because it enabled me to see my own self and that of others as a space—an internal, metaphorical, imagined, or virtual space—that can be entered and explored like you enter, explore, and travel through a real landscape that exposes its unexpected vistas as far as its shifting horizon permits. Some of the regions in this space are clearly visible and enlightened, while others are darker and unexplored.

I will use this theory to go deeper into a meaning-search of some destabilizing events in my life and invite you to do the same with events in your life. But what do I mean by "destabilizing events"? I mean events or circumstances which are loaded with strong positive or negative emotions. They reside in our memories for a long time and retain a certain vividness, even in their details. Despite their impressive character, they are in no way traumatic. Rather, they give us the feeling that they made us to what we are now. As challenges to ourselves and emotions, they can even be transformed from negative to positive experiences, depending on the personal meanings we add to them in the course of time. Stronger, as storytelling and meaning-making individuals, we transform them into something that they were not before. It is not so that while going through the exploration of destabilizing events, our lives become more stable. No, rather we become more equipped to deal with other destabilizing events that do not stop to appear in our travel through the developmental paths of our lives.

In the present book, this theory not only links our stories but also offers a clarifying perspective from which we explore *why* we are destabilized, *how* we respond to these events, and *what* we can learn from them.

After long deliberation with myself, I decided to write this book, which is of a more personal and spontaneous nature than all the works—books and articles in scientific journals—that I published earlier. It is an endeavor to bring the personal and the scientific together, which gives me, more than in previous periods, the opportunity to "show my own face" and to explore to what extent this can be valuable to readers who are willing to join me in this travel, which is, at the same time, a journey in their own emotional experiences.

Each of the chapters of the present book is written in the form of a "narrative triangle." I start writing about an event that I remember as deeply impressive and investigate its meaning. Then I present the theory, which helps to better understand the meaning of these events and their implications for my life. In the course of each chapter I offer you a series of questions and exercises that you can use to explore the meaning of influential events in your life and you do so in the light of the same theory. The combination of (a) events in my autobiography, (b) the theory, and (c) events in your autobiography assists us to understand our *particular* stories, as expressions of more *general* human processes and phenomena.

In chapter 1 I concentrate on the emergence of Dialogical Self Theory in close connection with some influential personal experiences. This conceptual framework is, like my own autobiography, not so much a theory which shows what people *are* but what they are *becoming*. It is a theory that emphasizes the potentials of individuals who give form to their own lives and contribute to that of others. During my studies I learned that the person is not only an *object* of study, but also a *subject* who is able to actively interrogate and explore him- or herself and even a *project* that is developed over time by a self that is able, in close collaboration with significant others, to give a meaningful response to the events of life from an original, agentic, and responsible (response-able) point of view. My intention in this chapter is to explore what happens when the self is seen not only as a metaphorical space but also as a "society of mind." According to this metaphor, the self has no purely autonomous existence "within" or "in itself" but is rather an extended space: it *participates* in the changes of the social environment and the society at large, while having, at the same time, the capacity to *respond* to these changes from one's own original point of view. One of the specific features of this theory is that it does not assume that the self is unified and centralized on *apriori* grounds, but rather multi-voiced and dialogical. In this chapter I will focus on those parts of the theory that will be used in the later chapters in order to explore significant autobiographical events and their personal meaning.

In Chapter 2, I tell about a period in my life (primary school) in which I failed, both in my achievements at school and in my contacts with peers. In this period I learned what it is to be a "real loser" or "to bite the dust." Then, I describe a simple but wonderful remark by one of my teachers that, as the beginning of the "thread of Ariadne," helped me to find my way back to self-worth. From a theoretical point of view, I will elaborate on these events by showing the power of "promoter positions," that is, internal resources or significant others which facilitate the self to develop to some higher level of integration. In the course of this chapter I present some exercises that challenge you to go back to some high and low points in your life. In one of them, you describe two areas in your life, one where you have the feeling that you are making progress and one in which you have the feeling of being in regress. Then, you receive instructions to compare the meaningfulness of the two areas so that possible tensions become visible. I will challenge you to give an appropriate answer to these tensions.

Chapter 3 starts with an intriguing dream I had, in many variations, more than a hundred times during my adult years. In the central part of that dream, I made a decision that I terribly regretted later because it resulted in an experience of desperate loss. I will analyze this dream in the context of several themes in art and literature: the *Fugit Amor* theme, as depicted by the sculptor August Rodin; the experience of Narcissus who was not able to reach his mirror image in the water, as poetically described in Ovid's metamorphoses; and the myth of the lost paradise. Then, I discuss the experience of unattainable love in the context of two basic motives that show up regularly in philosophical and psychological literature: agency (or the striving for self-maintenance and self-enhancement) and communion (or the longing for contact and union with something or somebody else). In the form of a circle, I present some significant *I*-positions that can be seen as expressions of these basic motives. Then, I provide you as a reader with a series of questions that lead to the placement of two of your significant *I*-positions in the circle: one that is prominent in your life and another which is less prominent or neglected. A brief analysis shows to what extent your positions can be seen as expressions of the two basic motives.

Chapter 4 starts with a description of my falling in love with the person who later became my present wife. I was wondering what happened with me after 43 years of marriage with my first wife. I found the answer in William James's (1902) *Varieties of Religious Experience*, in which he introduced the intriguing notion of "unstable equilibrium." This notion helped me to understand the phenomenon of "dominance reversal" that I did not only find in my research participants but also in my own falling in love: apparently I lived, for a long time, with a self in which particular *I*-positions were dominant over others. However, less visible and at a lower level of awareness there were other positions that were not fulfilled for a long time. They caused an increase in tension and even pressure in the self and produced a state of unstable equilibrium. My falling in love could be understood as a dominance reversal, implying that positions that were earlier at the background of the self moved, suddenly and with force, to the foreground, with the simultaneous suppression of positions that were hitherto dominant in the self-repertoire. In a different context I illustrate the phenomenon of dominance reversal in the life of a remarkable Dutch bishop who, after a period of intense media exposure, gave up his job and entered a monastery where he wanted to stay for the rest of his life. In the course of the chapter, you have the opportunity to investigate if you were ever involved in a situation that led to a dominance reversal or if you are presently in a state of unstable equilibrium. If so, I ask you to describe how you respond to this state.

Finally, in Chapter 5 I address a theme which I see as central to the functioning of self and society in our time: *coping with the experience of uncertainty*. I start this chapter by revealing that I lived, during my lifetime, in three "worlds": a traditional (my grandparents in a small village), modern (my study at school), and post-modern one (becoming member of an international network of scientists and practitioners). I focus on some differences between those worlds and I argue that in our globalizing society we live in these worlds not successively but simultaneously. Given this simultaneity, we are faced with tensions and contradictions between the different worlds that ask for dialogical answers. Elaborating on this view, I consider some situations in which uncertainty is a burden and other ones in which it is a gift. I go a step further by showing that uncertainty is even a *necessity*. I show how dealing with uncertainty is essential in different human achievement domains like art and science. I describe five reactions to uncertainty—retreat, opposition, conformity, intensification, and "dialogicality"—that can be observed in the personal, social and political arenas today. I will delineate how a dialogical reaction requires going *into* uncertainty rather than avoiding it. In this context, special attention is devoted to the significance of "tolerance of uncertainty" in a globalizing society. This leads to a series of exercises in which you have the opportunity to explore how you deal with different forms of uncertainty and in which ways tolerance of uncertainty can be productive in your own life.

In summary, as a personal-professional autobiography, this book is directed at the interface between author and audience. We both present autobiographical stories as part of a play of positions and counter-positions. The dialogical theory offers a *common language* for both parties to interrogate their stories and respond with adaptive answers to moments of destabilization. This creates the possibility of a theory-guided autobiographical self-exploration. The book invites both author and readers to tell and investigate their stories about destabilizing events in their lives and to travel through the spaces of the self in search of meaning.

The book starts with an overview of autobiographical events and significant memories. This overview offers a broader context for the subsequent chapters, so that they can be located as parts of an ongoing life story.

Autobiographical Events and Significant Memories

1937 (9 October): I was born as the oldest son of Mathieu Hermans (1908–1988), a baker in the center of Maastricht, in the south of The Netherlands, and Jeannette Spronck (1911–2005), the daughter of a farmer in Gronsveld, in the neighborhood of Maastricht. During my youth I lived alternatively in the city and in the village (for their specific cultures and their mutual tension see Chapter 5 of the present book).

1941: I hated going to nursery school because I wanted to stay permanently with my beloved mother. I used to cling myself to the foot of a heavy table in refusal of having to leave the house. Disabled as she was as the result of a failed hip surgery, she had the heavy task of tearing me away from the table and bringing me to school despite my protest.

1942: First accident: my 3–year old brother poured out, unaware of the danger, a strong hydrochloric acid over my head. Instinctively, I closed my eyes and mouth firmly: a narrow escape. During the next weeks, my hyperswollen face was like that of a monster and I remember that everybody was staring at me.

1944: I remember that I was in the street (Brusselsestraat in Maastricht) in September 1944 looking at the passing military army, soldiers of the American 30th Infantry Division "Old Hickory," who liberated my place of birth from the German occupation. I liked the American soldiers very much because they always had chewing gum in their pockets. I discovered a magic formula to get it. I said in broken English: "Mother poor, want chewing gum." It was never refused. It was my first played *I*-position.

1945: In the night of 31 December 1944–1 January 1945, some months after the liberation of the South of the Netherlands by the Americans, there was a great party in my father's bakery. Suddenly, a bomb was dropped from a passing airplane, which killed around 25 neighbors in their houses on the opposite side of the street. This was an extreme shock, particularly for those partygoers whose houses were affected by the disaster, knowing that their relatives were buried under the ruins. At that moment, I was sleeping in a cellar of the house and, awaken by the clash, remember vividly the sound of breaking windows. The next day, the beheaded body of one of the neighbors was found in the attic of our house. By the enormous air pressure it was catapulted in the air and fell down through the tiles of the roof.

1948: Second incident: My younger brother threw some of my papers out of the window of my room so that they were distributed on a glass roof of a lower part of our house. When I tried to recollect them, I slipped and fell through the glass with my head on the floor three meters lower. My relatives told me later that I was lying there and bleeding and crying for my mother. One of my father's employees picked me up with the intention of taking me to the family doctor who had his practice in the neighborhood. The driver of a passing-by car stopped and brought us to the emergency room. It was a narrow escape again.

1946: My original first name was "Berry." This was not a problem until there appeared a strip in the local newspaper with an ugly whale, named "Boerri-Berri," as the central character. From that time on, many people, both peers and adults, called me, smilingly and often in a ridiculing way, "Boorry-Berry." It made me feel marginalized and humiliated.

1947: I was bullied at school by my classmates and frequently ridiculed by my peers, by the teacher and by an uncle who tried to help me with my homework but without success. I was called a "dreamer." My performance went down dramatically, I had to repeat the class and lost all my self-esteem. I felt like a total outsider and reduced to "nothing" (for a more detailed story of that period and its impact on my life, see chapter 2).

1951: Admitted to the "gymnasium," the highest level of secondary education in the school system in my country. This admission followed after a considerable improvement of my performance in the final years of primary school. In the new school, I found myself, as the son of a baker, surrounded by sons of engineers, doctors, and professors. I tried to survive in this new situation by getting high grades.

Falling in love with José Jeunhomme, a girl who lived in the same street where I lived. I had regular contact with her during my adolescence and finally she became my girlfriend. However, the relationship ended after one year. She continued to appear in my dreams with angel-like qualities over a period of more than 50 years.

1952: Third accident: While sliding in the snow, I playfully took the cap of an older boy from his head while he was passing on a slide. Some moments later, I was on the same slide and noticed that he was behind me. At the end of the slide, I stopped by the wall of a house and he stabbed me my back with a knife. I remember the caring and sad face of my father holding my hand on our way to the hospital in an ambulance, when my breathing became shorter and shorter as the result of air coming into my body and pressing my lungs. However, in the emergency room the wound was treated successfully. This was another narrow escape.

1954: Although I did my best at school, I felt very opposed to the system with its authoritarian teachers who were very strict on disciplinary rules and who checked our presence in the church, obliged as we were to attend the mass with a minimum frequency of four times a week, in addition to Sundays. One time, when I was singing with a (too) low voice during a religious ceremony, the priest-teacher noticed me and sent me to the rector of the school. While he was yelling in my face, I showed my resistance just by looking into his eyes very directly and strongly. He got so upset that he dismissed me for one day from school and phoned my parents, a serious punishment at that time. This was a shocking event to me because I did not expect that my opposing behavior could have such a dramatic effect.

1958: Against my will, I had to join the military. After two months of introduction, I was not admitted to the officer training, to my great disappointment. Instead, I had to work as a "wash boss" in the dark cellar of a military building, sorting the dirty laundry of my fellow soldiers and later as a "line worker" connecting different telephones in the field with wires (although I was totally not technically inclined). During that time, I learned how to get on with colleagues of lower educational levels and I experienced their strong solidarity as group members.

1960–1965: Study of psychology at the University of Nijmegen, The Netherlands. During this study there was much emphasis on European philosophy and phenomenology, which received my life-long interest. At the same time, we were trained in psychometric and experimental approaches by young staff members who had visited the US at the beginning of their career. After some years of persistent effort, I got my master degree as the first student of my year.

1960: Falling in love with Els Jansen, whom I met at an institute for youth care in Lochem, where I did my first internship as part of my psychology study.

1961: I married Els Jansen, with whom I have two children: Matthieu (1962) and Desirée (1964). Via Desirée, we have two grandchildren: Dorothée (1989) and Camille (1992).

1967: Dissertation titled *Motivatie en Prestatie* (Motivation and achievement) with my professor Theo Rutten as promoter. From him I learned to give attention to the variety and richness of the phenomenal world and to describe it in clear and direct language.

1968: Construction of the Prestatie-Motivatie Test (Achievement Motivation Test). At present, more than two million copies have been sold. The Achievement Motive scale of this test and its research results were published in the *Journal of Applied Psychology*, 1970, *54*, 353–363.

1968: My first travel to the US, enabled by a grant received from the Nederlandse Organisatie voor Zuiver Wetenschapelijk Onderzoek [Dutch Organization for Pure Scientific Research]. It was the most impressive travel I ever made in my life. I visited Harvard University (David McClelland), Stanford University (Lee Cronbach), the Oregon Research Institute (Lewis R. Goldberg), and the Center for the Study of the Person (Carl Rogers). Most impressive, however, was the student revolution and the protest against the Vietnam War. Imagine: a student standing on the roof of a building of the University of Berkeley and giving a passionate speech for an audience of a thousand of students, while at the same time long-haired students were sitting on the stairs, playing their guitar (October, 1968). Or, a student-band walking through a water fountain, finally stopping at the institute of physics where they challenged the scientists to come out of their "holes" for a discussion…which they did (Stanford University, October 1968)!

1971: Construction of the Prestatie-Motivatie Test for children (Achievement Motivation Test for Children). More than two million copies were sold until now. Research with this test was published in Hermans, H. J. M., Ter Laak, J. J. F., & Maes, P. C. J. M. (1972). Achievement motivation and fear of failure in family and school. *Developmental Psychology, 6,* 520–528.

1972: Appointed as associate professor of personality psychology at the University of Nijmegen.

1974: The first Dutch publication on the Self-Confrontation Method (SCM): Hermans, H.J.M., *Waardegebieden en hun Ontwikkeling: Theorie en Methode van Zelfconfrontatie* [Value areas and their development: Theory and Method of Self-Confrontation]. Amsterdam: Swets & Zeitlinger.

1975: Starting to apply the Self-Confrontation Method in practice in cooperation with Els Hermans-Jansen who had an independent psychotherapeutic practice. As a co-therapist, I cooperated with her, applying new versions of the Self-Confrontation Method over the years. Els contributed significantly to many practical innovations of the method and has given a major boost to its further development.

1976–1977: Fellow of the *Netherlands Institute for Advanced Study in the Humanities and Social Sciences* (NIAS) in Wassenaar. I did not publish anything during that year, but it was a fertile period for discussion with fellow scientists and there was plenty time for volleyball and the creation of new ideas.

1980: I was appointed as full professor of personality psychology at the University of Nijmegen. The advantage was the large degree of autonomy and freedom of research, but I hated the frequent meetings.

1987: After some initial publications in American journals (1969 and 1970), I was writing exclusively in Dutch, in order to make the Self-Confrontation Method well-known in my country, both for scientists and practitioners. In 1987 I continued to write and publish in American and English journals:

Hermans, H. J. M. (1987a). Self as organized system of valuations: Toward a dialogue with the person. *Journal of Counseling Psychology, 34,* 10–19.

Hermans, H. J. M. (1987b). The dream in the process of valuation: A method of interpretation. *Journal of Personality and Social Psychology, 53,* 163–175.

Hermans, H. J. M., Hermans-Jansen, E., & Van Gilst, W. (1987). The *fugit amor* experience in the process of valuation: A self-confrontation with an unreachable other. *British Journal of Psychology, 78,* 465–481.

1992: The first psychological publication on the dialogical self:

Hermans, H. J. M., Kempen, H. J. G., & Van Loon, R. J. P., The dialogical self: Beyond individualism and rationalism. *American Psychologist, 47,* 23–33. This article was the basis for the later Dialogical Self Theory (2010).

I was invited to become First International Associate of the Society for Personology, USA.

Together with some colleagues, I established the Valuation Theory and Self-Confrontation Foundation, which created a training program for this theory and method.

1993: Lecture for mayors, scientists and artists in the presence of Queen Beatrix and Prince Klaus in the Royal Palace in Amsterdam. Stephen Toulmin and Catherine Bateson were the other speakers at this symposium.

1994: The quality of my research project (Valuation and Motivation) was rated as "excellent" by an international committee of scientists who had the task of evaluating all research programs of universities in the Netherlands. This evaluation was important to me as a recognition of my work in a psychological institute, where many colleagues used to consider me as a "hobbyist" who was doing "things" far removed from mainstream scientific psychology. In the next evaluation round (1999) my research program received the "excellent" rating again. As a result of these ratings, my work was finally recognized by my university colleagues.

1995: After a period of 20 years, in which we applied the Self-Confrontation Method in the psychotherapy practice of my first wife and colleague, Els Hermans-Jansen, we wrote a book on the Method in English:

Hermans, H.J.M., & Hermans-Jansen, E., *Self-Narratives: The Construction of Meaning in Psychotherapy.* New York: Guilford Press.

1997: Establishment of the *Nederlands Centrum voor de ZKM* (Netherlands Center for the SCM), a name which was later changed into *Vereniging voor ZKM-beoefenaars* (Association for SCM-practitioners). By 2011 the association had approximately 300 members.

1999: I travelled to India for a keynote address at a conference organized by the Osmania University in Hyderabad. I was impressed by the infinite variety of dresses, religions, and cultural traditions of the country and I could feel the mysticism of the far past.

Later in the same year: I lectured at the Swinburne Technological University in Melbourne, Australia, a continent of unlimited space.

2000: Death of my colleague and friend Harry Kempen with whom I used to discuss "everything" for more than 30 years.

First International Conference on the Dialogical Self in Nijmegen, organized by Michael Katzko. This was the beginning of a series of biennial international conferences in other countries.

2001: First special issue on the dialogical self in *Culture & Psychology*, *7* (3). Other special issues on the subject followed in *Theory & Psychology*, 2002, *12* (2), *Journal of Constructivist Psychology*, 2003, *16* (2), *Identity: An International Journal of Theory and Research*, 2004, *4* (4), *Counselling Psychology Quarterly*, 2006, *19* (1), *Journal of Constructivist Psychology*, 2008, *21* (3), *Studia Psychologica,* 2008, *6* (8), *Theory & Psychology,* 2010, *20* (3), *New Directions in Child and Adolescent Psychology* (in preparation), and *Journal of Constructivist Psychology* (in preparation).

2002: I received the decoration as "Knight in the Order of the Netherlands Lion" on behalf of the Queen for exceptional scientific achievements in the service of society.

Retirement as professor of psychology at the University of Nijmegen after 40 years of research in psychology (however, continuing my research and writing at home).

Establishment of the International Society for Dialogical Science (ISDS).

Second Conference on the Dialogical Self in Ghent, Belgium, organized by Leni Verhofstadt-Denève.

2004: Third International Conference on the Dialogical Self in Warsaw, organized by Katarzyna Stemplewska and Piotr Oles.

Falling in love with Agnieszka Konopka, who participated in the conference in the period of finishing her dissertation on emotions at the Cardinal Wyszynski University in Warsaw. I describe the impact of this event as a "revolution" in my personal self in Chapter 4 of the present book.

Launching a new journal: *International Journal for Dialogical Science* (IJDS). One of its innovative features is that publication of a peer-reviewed article in this journal leads automatically to membership of the *International Society for Dialogical Science* (ISDS).

2006: Fourth International Conference on the Dialogical Self in Braga, Portugal, organized by Miguel Goncalves.

I wrote the book *Dialoog en Misverstand* [Dialogue and Misunderstanding] which was used by Herman Wijfels during the preparation of the Dutch government in 2007.

2007: Agnieszka Konopka and I established the *International Institute for the Dialogical Self* with the intention to develop methods for application in coaching and counseling. One of the methods is the "composition work," which is inspired by Japanese gardens seen as "mindscapes." The method makes use of stones representing I-positions in the space of the self as an artistic composition.

Honorary member of the *Vereniging voor ZKM-Beoefenaars* (Association for SCM-Practitioners).

2008: I married Agnieszka Konopka, who had finished a dissertation on the psychology of emotions in 2006.

Fifth International Conference on the Dialogical Self in Cambridge, UK, organized by Alex Gillespie and Tania Zittoun.

2009: Agnieszka established the *Dialogical Self Network* in order to further stimulate the practical implication of the Theory. The network has brought together colleagues from 36 countries (as of 2012) with the intention to enable researchers and practitioners to inform each other about their work and to stimulate their cooperation.

Travel to Japan for a keynote at the Conference of the *Japanese Psychological Association* in Kyoto. Together with Agnieszka I gave a workshop on the practical implications of Dialogical Self Theory. Agnieszka and I visited several Buddhist temples and rock gardens and a Shinto temple (for more details see Jones & Morioka, 2011).

2010: Publication of the book:

Hermans, H.J.M., & Hermans-Konopka, A., *Dialogical Self Theory: Positioning and Counter-Positioning in a Globalizing Society.* Cambridge, UK:

Cambridge University Press. In his praise of the book Jeffrey Arnett (Clark University, USA) said: "The dialogical self is among the most important and original new theories in the social sciences in the past 20 years..."

Sixth International Conference on the Dialogical Self in Athens, Greece, organized by Stavros Charalambides.

2011: I travelled through South Africa where I lectured at the University of KwaZulu-Natal in Pietermaritzburg, the University of Fort Hare in Alice (where Mandela and other black leaders have studied), and the Rhodes University in Grahamstown.

2012: Publication of the *Handbook of Dialogical Self Theory*, edited by Hubert Hermans and Thorsten Gieser, Cambridge, UK: Cambridge University Press. The book has 29 contributions by authors from 15 countries, including an epilogue by philosopher Shaun Gallagher.

Honorary Associate of the *Taos Institute*.

Seventh International Conference on the Dialogical Self in Athens, Georgia, USA, organized by Bob Fecho.

Chapter One

The Emergence of
Dialogical Self Theory

Every perfect traveler always creates the country where he travels.

Nikos Kazantzakis

In this chapter I want to explain how I developed, together with my colleagues, the Dialogical Self Theory which played a central role in my scientific and professional life. I will not do so in an "objective" way with the "distant look" of a scientist. Rather, I will share what happened in my personal life, as it has been closely related to my professional development. I came to realize that significant life events have a strong influence on one's development as a scientist or professional. The "personal factor" is typically hidden in the thousands of papers and books that appear every year in the social sciences and other fields while it has conscious or unconscious influence on the selection, formation, and development of our thoughts and projects in which we are involved as professionals.[1]

A theory is never developed in isolation. There are always other people—scientists, philosophers, or artists—who creep into your mind where they meet your own thoughts and feelings, which then lead to unpredictable "products" as hybrid combinations of external inspirations and the internal responses of our minds.

Moreover, when you become involved in the development of a theory, method, or approach, there is always a history in the background, something you did in the previous period of your life or career. You want to elaborate on something, to do it better than before, to do it differently, or turn your back to it forever! Before you started to think about the subject, there were already forerunners who had thoughts and ideas related, in one way or another, to yours.

In this text I will tell my personal story about the experiences which led me, in rather unpredictable ways, to the point in my professional career where I'm now. I will sketch the road which I travelled through the decades with its sudden turns, unexpected vistas, and obstacles that I tried to tackle in more or less successful ways. In doing so, I'm aware that there is no end-point in this story, which develops rather like an "unfinished symphony."

THE CONSTRUCTION OF AN ACHIEVEMENT MOTIVATION TEST AND MY INCREASING RESISTANCE TO IT

In 1964, one year before my master degree, I did an internship in the Dutch State Mines (DSM) in the south of the Netherlands, in a period when the company was faced with a huge problem: the end of the coalmine industry in our country. For several years the business was making a loss. The competition by alternative fuels, like oil, gas, and cheaper coal from other countries, created an irreversible situation. Thousands of jobs were at stake and the company was faced with the threat of mass unemployment and decline of the economic status of the whole area. However, DSM had a chemical industry which was more profitable than the mining industry. Therefore, it was decided to invite underground mineworkers to participate in a retraining project that would enable them to work as chemical craftsmen. The top management asked the psychological service of the company to investigate which psychological factors were predictive for retraining success. I did my internship in the period that the report of this investigation was available. It impressed me to read that motivation had a stronger predictive value than intelligence. Apparently, successful workers were not the most intelligent, but those with the strongest motivation to achieve. On the basis of these results, psychologists became interested in the research work of David McClelland and John Atkinson, the heroes of the achievement motive. However, after some try-outs they complained that the Thematic Apperception Test procedure, the main assessment instrument, had a complex and time-consuming scoring system and was, from a psychometric perspective, not very reliable. I noticed that, at least in my country, there was no questionnaire method available for the measurement of the achievement motive. So, I decided to make one.

I was lucky to have a supervisor, Aat Boon van Ostade, who had devised a statistical method for grouping data, called "iterative cluster analysis." I applied this method to hundreds of multiple choice questions I had formulated to measure the achievement motive and two closely related traits, debilitating and facilitating anxiety. The cluster analysis proved to be very useful because

I found that the three traits were statistically independent from each other. My next step was to perform a series of studies in order to investigate the reliability and validity of the scales. This formed, together with an extensive literature review, the basis of my dissertation which I defended on November 3rd 1967 at the University of Nijmegen.

Publishing a Test or Not?

There was another person who facilitated my dissertation work, Lewis Goldberg, who worked as a Fulbright professor at the University of Nijmegen, 1966–1967, and who later became well-known for his work on the Big Five personality taxonomy. During his time in Nijmegen he became interested in my dissertation work which led to several illuminating discussions about psychology in the USA. I was walking around with the idea to distribute the test via an official publisher, convinced as I was about its value for research and practice. I was curious about Lewis' opinion. So, I went to his room and posed the question. Leaning backwards on his chair, he was silent for some moments. Then, he took his pipe from his mouth and said to my surprise: "Hubert, I strongly dissuade you from publishing a test." Then it was my turn to react with silence. However, there was not any thoughtfulness but rather confusion on my part. I asked: "Why do you dissuade me?" He answered: "I have seen quite some colleagues in my country who published a test in the beginning of their career and became so identified with it that it blocked their further career as a scientist." I left his room with some uncertainty but it finally did not change my plan. My ambition to publish the test was too strong. I just wanted it and nobody could stop me from doing it. So, I took the train to Amsterdam, together with the head of my department, Gerard Brenninkmeijer, and found the publisher Swets & Zeitlinger who were willing to publish and market the instrument. Over the years, many organizations used the test for selection purposes and educational institutions applied it in order to determine the motivation and fear of failure of their students.

When I think back to Goldberg's advice, his dissuasion made some sense, however, for a very different reason than he suggested. Some years after my dissertation, I lost interest in the field of achievement motivation and, by implication, also in the test. Yet, the publisher and test users continued to haunt me and make revisions of the test. In fact, I did this several times over the decades but I never did it with real pleasure. Even when other people took over part of the job, I was always involved in one way or another in the project because I was the author. Since many colleagues in my country know about the test, I continued to be associated with the test: "Hubert Hermans? Ah, from the motivation test!" This imposed an identity on me which did not fit at all to my later work, which in some respects was far removed from my earlier achievement motivation research. Despite these disadvantages, I cannot say that the publication of the test was a serious obstacle to my further scientific development. The fact was that I became so involved in my later projects that I could leave the achievement motivation project behind me without much connection.

Travel to the USA and My Opposition to the Achievement Motive

As a result of our discussions and his interest in my dissertation work, Goldberg invited me to come to the USA and visit his Oregon Research Institute in Eugene. A grant from the Netherlands Organization of Pure Scientific Research enabled me to make a round-trip in the USA for three months in 1968. From a historical point of view, this was a special year with some remarkable and even shocking events: The assassination of Bob Kennedy (I saw his pictures exposed at several memorial places in the country); Martin Luther King being shot dead at the Lorraine Motel in Memphis, Tennessee (when I visited this motel/museum in 2004, I saw the coffee cup from which he was drinking just before he was murdered); the U.S. presidential election with republican Richard Nixon defeating his democratic opponent Hubert Humphrey; and the U.S. spacecraft Apollo 8 entering the orbit around the moon which enabled the astronauts to see, as the first humans, the far side of the moon while reading from Genesis.

As part of this travel, I spent five weeks at the Oregon Research Institute where I learned not only how American psychologist are doing rigorous research on the basis of big grants, but also how some of them had the freedom to combine their psychological work with political aspirations. One of the directors, Paul Hoffman, was running for the position of mayor of Eugene. Some weeks before the elections, all researchers and employees received a button with the words "Hoffman for Mayor" which everybody seemed to wear without any sign of protest. As a young scientist I was going every day to the institute with the button prominently on my jacket, astonished about the apparent lack of separation of science and politics to which I was so used to in my own country.

It was the first time in my life that I experienced that travelling is, at the same time, a journey into the space of one's own self. One of the more intense emotions I had during this travel was when I was sitting on my own in a Greyhound bus somewhere in California. I felt a strong anger: anger at my university, anger at my superiors, and most of all, anger at my own work on motivation which I felt was uncritically conforming not only to mainstream psychology but, at the same time, to the main values of our (achieving) society. Instead of letting myself become incarcerated in the prison of societal norms, I wanted to be free and do what I wanted *myself*, and *not* following the expectations of my university, fund-suppliers and society as a whole.

Writing these lines, I realize, after so many years, that there was something paradoxical in this anger. I was never so free as during this travel. I could do what I wished and go where I wanted to go. I did not have any obligations. I could make the travel as a reward for the motivation work which I despised so strongly at the moment of most freedom. Much later, I understood this anger better in a discussion with a colleague-sociologist. Talking about revolutions, he said: "The revolutionist is the climber, not the person at the bottom." The people who have tasted at least some freedom, want to have more of it because they *know* on the basis of their own experience what freedom really is. In contrast, people who have never experienced any form of societal freedom, don't know what it is and therefore will not start a revolution. This is reflected in a statement which is attributed to the philosopher Kierkegaard: "Even when the whole world knows something, but I have not yet experienced it … then it has not any meaning for me."

Certainly, another powerful factor in my reorientation was the increasing attraction that humanistic psychology had on me and many others. The names of Abraham Maslow and Carl Rogers had almost magical connotations at that time. Wherever I came during my travel, people talked about the Esalen Institute, a residential community and retreat center in Big Sur, California. The Institute aimed at the full realization of "human potential," based on the belief that people have much more possibilities in themselves than they have actually realized. Many people at that time, including psychologists, philosophers, artists, and physicists, were engaged in this movement driven by the idea that there was a great deal of uncultivated potential in people that was lying largely untapped. Bringing these hidden treasures to the surface promised a life filled with creativity, happiness and fulfillment.

The fascination about human potential was strongly conflicting with my work on achievement motivation, which was based on the paradigm of "individual differences," which assumes that people can be described and compared on the basis of characteristics, like traits, motives, or schemas. While the human potential movement is interested in what a person *can be*, the individual difference paradigm is focused on what the person *actually is*.

I became more and more under the spell of the promise of human potential, because I actually experienced it. Traveling from the east coast to the west coast and back, I could go where I wanted and leave. When I had looked around and met some people at a particular place, I booked another flight as soon as I felt the need to experience something new. I noticed in myself not only a clear difference between what was new and what was habitual but became increasingly sensitive for the moments a new environment lost its initial fresh character and changed into something habitual. These were the moments my own behavior became a "custom," the beginning of an automatism, the start of just repetition and this became something to "avoid."

Approaching California as the promised land, I visited Palo Alto, Stanford, San Francisco, Los Angeles successively, and finally the place which I expected to find the holy grail, La Jolla, where Carl Rogers had recently established his "Institute for the study of the *person.*" Yes, the name of this institute had an appeal to me because here the "person" was central rather than *"personality"* that led psychologists to objectify, analyze and, by implication, confirm people in their existing traits rather than stimulate them in their growth. I could understand, some years later, Rae Carlson (1971), who wrote an article with the title "Where is the person in personality research?"[2]

After some very inspiring talks with colleagues of Carl Rogers (he himself was not there), I felt a sudden urge to go to Salt Lake City in order to get an impression of the life of the Mormons and to listen to the famous Mormon Tabernacle Choir. When I was preparing my travel, I met a student whom I never met before. I told him my plan and he proposed to bring me to the airport with his car (typical of the sixties was that you could meet a stranger with whom you became familiar in just one brief talk; the pervasive community feeling facilitated a quick transition from stranger to friend). The same day I arrived at my destination where I visited the well-known temple, listened to the choir and left after two days for a visit noisy Chicago, a striking contrast to the heavenly landscapes of California.

I share these details just to illustrate that this travel strongly *enlarged the space* in myself: I could follow my impulses and fulfill many desires. I visited new places and met people who enriched me with inspiring ideas. I re-experienced my past again and felt attracted to music that I loved during my adolescence. I was swimming on December 5th in a swimming pool in the sun in La Jolla while it was freezing in my own country. And I had *plenty time* for all of this. All these experiences (and many more) facilitated that my life progressed, at that time, beyond the usual and the habitual. It lifted me up to higher energy levels. I stepped out of the routines of my daily life, which cleared my vision to an unusual degree. Marcel Proust saw this very sharply when he said, "The real voyage of discovery consists not in seeing new landscapes, but in having new eyes." In other words, I experienced the human potential movement not just as a view of life and not just as an interesting professional experience, but *I felt it in my body.*

Does this mean that the travel was a continuous being "on top of the world"? Certainly not. I was three full months alone in a strange country, with a language which I only partly commanded. After my visit to Eugene, I went to Palo Alto where I lived for about four weeks in a dark hotel without a restaurant and without any social life. From there I went on a daily basis with a rented bike to Stanford University, where I talked to several people without feeling real contact with anyone. I felt more and more alone and lonely. Then, I met a woman who was a staff member at this university and I fell in love with her. However, it was quite an unhappy love affair. It became my first *fugit amor* experience: feeling strong love for a person who was, at the same time, unreachable.[3]

After walking around as a lonely wolf for some time, I met a co-student, an Indian woman, who invited me for a dinner with her and her husband. She introduced me to other students and gradually I got a feeling of connectedness with my social environment. In fact, the American travel experience brought

---

EXERCISE 1.1
This exercise aims to explore the relationship between making a travel in the physical world and making a journey in yourself. The assumption is that not only the environment around you is spatial but also the self functions as a land-scape of the mind through which you can move.

Question 1
Can you describe in a few lines an impressive travel which influenced the way you live in your internal space?

_____
_____
_____

Question 2
Can you describe the kind of change which took place in yourself (short-term or long-term, superficial or deep?)

_____
_____
_____

Question 3
What did you do with this experience? If you did not do something with it, what do you imagine you *could* do?

_____
_____
_____

me to both higher and lower points of experience than ever before in my adult life. It evoked in me a life-long interest in the "richness experience" with special attention to its contrasts, opposites, and fields of tensions.

FROM TRAIT PSYCHOLOGY TO PERSONAL MEANING IN SELF-CONFRONTATION

The American travel experience had, in fact, a deep influence on my life and career. It put me entirely out of my "comfort zone" and it brought energies to the surface which I did not have before, certainly not in that degree of intensity. I had the feeling that this was not simply an interesting travel but a profound experience loaded with personal meaning. I had to *do* something with it. It should have consequences. It had even a moral significance. I was wondering what the nature of its meaning was. I cannot find another word to describe it than with the concept of "call." During and after the travel there was something in me, a kind of dedication that said: "I want to make this experience productive and unfold its command." However, I did not know how! After all, it gave me a direction. It was heading to the notion of "personal meaning."

When I returned home before Christmas 1968, I took up my normal duties and continued to work on my regular projects. One of them was to construct an achievement motivation test for children, which was published in 1971. In the period between the end of 1968 and the end of 1971 I did not do anything that was related to my experience in America. I worked on a book and manual for the Prestatie-Motivatie Test voor kinderen (Achievement Motivation Test for children), which was published at the end of 1971. After the publication, I participated in a conference on achievement motivation at the Starnberger See at the south of Munich, Germany, organized by my colleague Heinz Heckhausen, a productive and influential researcher on "Leistungsmotiva-tion" (achievement motivation). It was during that conference that two things happened. First of all, visiting this conference convinced me that I was not the kind of person to stay in the field of achievement motivation. I felt no longer "at home" in the area of investigation. Secondly, I got an idea to construct an entirely different approach, which I later called, the Self-Confrontation Method (SCM).[4] The kernel of the idea was to ask people what they find important in their lives and what they find meaningful when they look at their past, present, and expected future. Instead of providing to respondents a set of pre-fabricated items with multiple choices, reducing their contribution to marking one of the answers, I wanted to bring persons deeper into their own experiences and to explore, together with them, the personal meaning of significant events and circumstances in their lives.

So, I developed a set of open questions referring to the past (e.g., "Has there been anything of major significance in your past that still continues to exert a strong influence on you?), to the present (e.g., "Is there anything in your present life that is of major importance to you or exerts a significant influence on you?), and to the future (e.g., "Do you foresee anything that will be of great importance for or exert a major influence on your future life?"). These and other questions were read aloud by psychologist and client sitting side by side, in order to reflect a situation of cooperation rather than objectification. The client was then invited to give his associations to the question, which led finally, with the assistance of the psychologist, to a sentence formulated and authorized by the client. The sentences were written down on small cards so that they could be shifted, compared and ordered in groups. I called such a sentence "valuation" because it had personal value to the client as part of an intensified self-reflection.

During the construction of the method, I was aware of the great importance of *feelings* for the area of personal meaning. Therefore, I decided to explore the affective meaning of the different valuations. I did this by providing the client with a set of positive (e.g. joy, enjoyment, inner calm) and negative feelings (e.g., anxiety, powerlessness, disappointment) with the question to indicate to what extent a particular valuation was associated with a particular feeling. The intensity of the feeling was indicated by using a 0–5 scale. This procedure resulted in a matrix of valuations X feelings and allowed for a series of quantitative indices that revealed the affective organization of the valuation system.

In order to calculate these affective indices, my colleague Willem van Gilst and I developed a series of computer programs that that enabled us to calculate them easily and efficiently. One week after the self-investigation, I discussed the results of the investigation in such a way that it led to action plans formulated on the basis of the investigation, which allowed a gradual transition between assessment and change. After some weeks or months a second investigation followed that allowed the client and me to inspect the changes in the content and organization of the valuation system. In the meantime sessions with the client took place to give direction to the actions that had resulted from the initial self-investigation.

The first person who started to work with the SCM in practice was my first wife Els Hermans-Jansen who worked as a psychotherapist in an independent practice. We had intensive discussions about each client, which led to many new ideas that were then applied in investigations with new clients. One of our observations was that there were two feelings which were quite different from each other but both are very relevant to the lives of many clients, self-esteem and love. We elaborated on these two feelings by distinguishing between two basic motives: the striving for self-assertion (S-motive) and the longing for contact and union with the other (O-motive). We then added an extra set of feelings specifically referring to these motives. The S-motive was represented, not only by the experience of self-esteem but also by the feeling of pride, strength, and self-confidence), while for the O-motive the feelings of care, tenderness, and intimacy were added to the feeling of love. This enabled us to determine for every valuation to what extent it had an S-quality, an O-quality, or a combination of both. We found out that the two motives were in most of our clients extremely useful, not only to understand where their strengths are and where their affective connections are, but also in which direction they wanted to develop themselves in the future.

Working as a co-therapist with Els Hermans-Jansen allowed me to listen to clients at the moments they had arrived at significant turning points in their lives and every investigation was like an adventurous journey in the world of another person. While in the trait approach I had the feeling that I looked at people at the outside, the more personal approach of the SCM allowed me to go *into* the experiential world of another person which was invisible for any objectifying instrument.

I had the feeling that in my professional journey I had made some significant steps. In at least three respects, the SCM was different from my trait-oriented approach of the years before. First, the method was open so that there was space for clients to introduce their own stories and concerns on the basis of open questions and formulate them in their own words. Second, clients could bring in anything that was of personal value to them. The achievement motivation test was—in terms of the philosopher Eduard Spranger—limited to theoretical values (referring to study) or economical values (referring to achievements in work), while the SCM allowed clients to bring in a broader range of values, including social, political, esthetic, and religious concerns. In a sense, it is a more "holistic" instrument. Third, and most important, the SCM was based on a cooperative relationship with the client rather than an objectifying relationship, which was so typical of the traditional assessment instruments, including my own achievement motivation test.

After some years of developing the method and its applications, we established in 1992 a foundation which offered a training program in the SCM for practitioners, with important contributions by Els Hermans-Jansen, Margaret Poulie, and Rens van Loon who gave the initial push to the program. In 1997 when an increasing number of practitioners started to apply the method in their practice, one of our students, Henk de Lijster, took the initiative to establish an official association which aimed at not only the protection of the professional interests of its members, but also offered additional workshops and training programs.

The Importance of My Daily Notes for
My Personal and Professional Development

In the period of developing the SCM, I started in 1974 to make notes, typically on a daily basis, about my personal and professional experiences, observations, and more or less crazy impulses and thoughts. My notes, a kind of diary, simply referred to anything. It could be about an interesting article that I had read, a talk with my wife, friend or colleague, an emotional experience or the sudden memory of an event which took place many years ago.

At the moment I'm writing this text, I have arrived at notebook number 183, each of them having 100 pages. I have noticed that these books became not only more detailed over the years but also more important from an affective point of view. Why? When going back to my notes in previous months, years, decades, I found out that I would forget more than 90% of all things I had reported. Even when I remember anything without my notes, it is much less detailed, precise, and vivid as described. So, they became a kind of external memory to which I can return at any moment. It is a good feeling to have them available because memory (or memorizing) revises, distorts, and simplifies events without being aware of it.

But there is more. The notebooks became a form of systematic self-reflection over time and also a dialogue with myself. I experience things *twice*: one time in reality and the second time, going back into memory, thoughts and imagination. Typically, my reflective memories *add* personal meanings to the events which were not there before. During the writing I discover relationships with other notes or I just see new connections at the moment of writing. Also at a deeper emotional level this re-experience is significant. Writing about an emotional experience is at the same time going into this experience again, which helps strengthening the ownership of the emotion and also to take some distance from emotions, particularly negative ones, when they become disorganizing.

Typically, when I'm preparing a book or an article, I start reading all my notes which refer to the main themes. I have numbered the pages and made an electronic file with key terms (e.g., anxiety, opposites, manicheism, William James). Dependent on the theme of the text I'm writing, I go with a searching program to the relevant key terms which leads me to the pages in the written notebooks where they are discussed. Going through the notes over years and even decades is often digging into a goldmine: searching and searching, but suddenly finding some material which gives an "aha-erlebnis." The only thing to do is to clean and polish it.

I was wondering what happens when making notes and why it became so relevant to me, as it is for many writers of diaries. What is significant is to write the notes on paper. This goes much more slowly than typing. Paper and pencil writing forces you to slow down your thoughts. This deceleration creates "a space between the lines" where unexpected thoughts, memories and even emotions can come in, which would be lost in case of higher speed. It is like a person who is talking very quickly, but being insensitive to new things which *could* come when he would be silent for some moments in between. Slowing down talking can have the same effect. Ludwig Wittgenstein understood this very well when, in the beginning of a lecture, he could take some 10 minutes for the formulation of what he saw as a "good question."

Making notes made me aware of the relativity of what you find "important." At the present moment I may have a certain view on a particular matter. Going back into my notes, I may find a different emphasis on the same thing or even a contrasting view on the subject. It is as if I meet another person who is actually the "same" person as I am. But meeting this person in his "alterity," broadens my view of the moment, a process which can also take place when you have an innovative talk with a colleague or friend. Becoming engaged in this process made me aware of the multiplicity of my identity and showed me that I'm another-to-myself. This juxtaposition of temporally distributed experiences broadened my horizon beyond the necessarily limited view of the present moment.

The Emergence of Dialogical Self Theory

In the final decade of the previous century, I felt increasingly uneasy with the Self-Confrontation Method to which I had devoted much energy from 1971 onward. The reason was that I became gradually interested in the wider implications of the process of dialogue, particularly in the self functioning in a dialogical way. Certainly, in my SCM period I had already published articles in which the notion of dialogue was explicitly mentioned. For example, the article entitled "Self as organized system of valuations: Toward a dialogue with the person," published in the *Journal of Counseling Psychology* (Hermans, (1987a), already referred explicitly to the concept. Without any doubt, there were already quite some dialogical elements in the SCM, for example, the openness of the method for the specific experiences formulated in the client's own words, seeing the client as a colleague or co-investigator rather than as an object of assessment or study, and discussing in a profound way the results of the investigation with ample space for the client's interpretations.

Yet, from a dialogical point of view, there were missing elements in the original construction of the SCM and its underlying valuation theory. The theory had no explicit place for the *other*, an indispensable component for any dialogical view. Moreover, the SCM invited to make a movement *inward* and functioned as an act of introspective self-reflection on the basis of which the client's growth was stimulated, and ideal which was not very different from Maslow's notion of "self-actualization" and Rogers' ideas about "fully functioning." Connected with these points, the approach had no vision on the place of the self in a broader *societal and historical context*.

The prolific chapter on the self, written by William James (1890), had a great impact on my thinking, already in the time when I started to work on the SCM. I read and reread the chapter several times and noticed that James introduced an idea, the *extension* of the self, that would have far reaching significance for the emergence of the later Dialogical Self Theory. James made clear that the self is not located inside the skin but extended to the environment. So, not only one's thoughts and feelings (*Me*) are belonging to the self but also that which the person calls his or her own (*Mine*), like my body, my father, my mother, my children, and even my opponent belongs to the self in a broadened sense of the term. I saw the extended self as a great step forward as it went beyond the Cartesian dualistic conception in which the self (res cogitans) and the environment (res extensa), including the other person, were seen as separate entities.

I could pursue this idea of an extended self further by reading Bakhtin's (1984) book on Dostoyewski, where he introduced the intriguing metaphor of the "polyphonic novel." The basic idea of this novel is that it is composed of a number of independent and mutually opposing viewpoints embodied by characters involved in dialogical relationships. Each of its characters is seen as "ideologically authoritative and independent," that is, each of them is perceived as the author of his or her own view of the world, rather than an object of Dostoyevsky's all-encompassing artistic vision. The characters are capable of standing not just below their creator but *beside* him, disagreeing with the author, even rebelling against him. The characters are not subordinated to Dostoyevsky's view but have their own voice and tell their own story. This development in the novelistic literature marks a revolution against the traditional idea of the "omniscient narrator."

I noticed that in the metaphor of the polyphonic novel there are two elements which go beyond James's conception of the extended self: the *independence* of the characters and the fact that they have a *voice*. The idea of a *self as dialogically extended to an independent other* was the road I wanted to go in formulating a new theory. In doing so, I realized that the other could never *entirely* escape my construction of him or her. Nevertheless, I saw this road as particularly promising because it had the potential of extending the self to a broader societal and historical context.[5]

My Cooperation with Harry Kempen

In the beginning of the project on the dialogical self I have cooperated intensely with my dear colleague Harry Kempen who died in 2000. Co-authored by him

and Rens van Loon, I wrote the first publication on the dialogical self, published in the *American Psychologist* in 1992. Harry and I had met already in
1965 when he was staff member of the Department of Culture and Religion of
the University of Nijmegen. This department was founded by my teacher, professor Han Fortmann, who strongly influenced me when I attended his lectures
about cultural psychology in the sixties. Harry and I had incidental talks in the
beginning of our contact, but they strongly increased in the period of our cooperation on the dialogical self. The most striking of our talks was that they were,
so to speak, about *everything*. That is, we did not simply talk about "interesting
things" but rather our energies met in a way that anything became interesting.
It was a way of looking at phenomena rather than the phenomena themselves.
There were no limits or boundaries in our talks. Harry could come in with a
review article of recent developments in sociology and the next day with a
book on the art of beer drinking. The two topics had no relationship but they
became intriguing, and sometimes even related, *by* the following interchange.
The main difference between us was that he was always moving very broadly
while I was more going into depth. He went every morning to the library and
always found something which was often relevant to running projects, while I
preferred to retreat to my working room at home in order to concentrate on an
article or book. We agreed that he was a "leveler" who tended to go to all sides
and connect everything with everything while I was more a "sharpener" who
was striving to clarify newly acquired information and included it, or not, as
part of a developing theoretical framework.[6]

FROM GROWTH TO DIALOGICAL TENSION:
THE EMERGENCE OF A THIRD POSITION

Without any doubt, the construction and development of the SCM was
strongly influenced by my interest in humanistic psychology and the human potential movement of the 60th. Dialogical Self Theory, as a later
development, embraced the idea that the presence of the other is more than
an external condition that facilitates or obstructs inborn potentials. In its
manifestation of the other-in-the-self (my imagined father, mother, colleague,
opponent, or cultural group which has some personal meaning for me) it is
rather an essential defining factor of the self as extended to its environment.
In this environment there are always actual others, individuals and groups,
who bring in new elements in the self and correct, revise, and broaden it
beyond existing structures. In this quality the other in the self functions as a
fertile soil for *tensions* in the self and, at the same time, forms a basis of its
further development. Let me illustrate this with an example of my own life.

Early in my life I became aware that I was a dreamer, not because I knew that I *was*, but because other people told me. At primary school not only my peers but also some of my teachers called me, sometimes smilingly, sometimes in a ridiculing way, the "sleeper" or the "dreamer." As a result I felt different from others and even an outsider. This did not stop my behavior and I did not become an "extravert." Instead, my response was to withdraw into myself even more than before and create there my own world. However, I wanted to find a way to survive at school and later, to find a place in society. Moreover, I wanted to keep the love of my parents who appreciated a good performance at school. So, I felt over the years in a field of tension between my position as a dreamer with a private fantasy world (going to the inside of myself) and my position as a recognition seeker who was ambitious enough to achieve something that would be rewarded by the love from my parents and the appreciation of my teachers (going to the outside world). In this sense my parents, teachers and peers entered myself as "external positions" and asked there for some *answer.*

For many years this tension between the "internal" and the "external" continued to be there but it remained largely unresolved. However, the tension became more productive when, in the last period of my university study, I was permitted to write a master thesis of my own choice and, later, to start a dissertation project of my own preference. While my primary school, high school and beginning of the psychology study gave me space for developing my recognition seeker *only*, the later period gave some opportunity to give expression to the energy of the dreamer who had remained latent in myself for many years.

The *real* moment of bringing the dreamer and the recognition seeker together as two "equal partners" was the period in which, after my travel in America, I took, and received, the freedom to give the dreamer in myself new space: the construction of the Self-Confrontation Method. The passion which came over me when I was working on this project can be understood as emanating from a "third position" in which two initially conflicting positions, the dreamer and the recognition seeker, went together in forming a coalition that was able to reconcile the initial conflict. I learned from this experience that motivation to achieve something is particularly strong when initially conflicting *I*-positions can be brought together at some higher level of integration. At that level, the conflicting positions reached, in terms of negotiation, a win-win solution. These experiences and their exploration on a theoretical level, led me to think about motivation in a more dynamic and *dialogical* way with a starting point very different from my initial trait-oriented approach of achievement motivation.

How would I name this third position? I don't know a better word than to call it a "creative position." I do this because creative work has two elements: "creativity" which in my case gave space to the dreamer and "work"

EXERCISE 1.2
This exercise is intended to explore a conflict between two *I*-positions (e.g., I as professional vs. I as a family member or I as a looking for adventure vs. I as in need of safety, or any other conflict you have experienced in your life).

Question 1
Can you describe the two positions in your own words?

Position 1:

_____
_____
_____

Position 2:

_____
_____
_____

Question 2
Can you describe the nature of the conflict between the two positions?

_____
_____
_____

Question 3
Was it possible for you to develop a third position which was able to reconcile the conflict while, at the same time, using the energies of both position as part of a new combination? What name would you give to that position? (if this did not take place at the time of the conflict, could you try to formulate such a reconciling position in retrospect. So, what you *could* have done to realize such a third position?)

_____
_____
_____

Question 4
Can you describe your experience with this third position? What did it give you and what did you do with it as part of your personal or professional life?

_____
_____
_____

which leads to a contribution to society that gives, in one way or another, its positive or negative feedback. However, what I call my creative position has had a special meaning for my development both as a person and professional. It gave me not only a chance to develop my work over the decades but also resulted in some rewarding contacts with friends and colleagues in different parts of the world. Therefore, I would call this position a "promoter position" as it has stimulated my social, scientific, and artistic development over the years. A special feature of a promoter position is that it stimulates the development of a broader range of more specific internal and external positions of the self and brings them to a higher level of integration (for a more extensive treatment of a promoter position and my experience with it, see Chapter 2).

LATER DEVELOPMENT: *I*-POSITIONS AND THEIR TRANSCENDENCE

In the year 2010 the book *Dialogical Self Theory: Positioning and Counter-Positioning in a Globalizing Society* (2010) was published, which I wrote together with Agnieszka Hermans-Konopka. In this book we brought together not only a diversity of literature around the theory published between 1992 and 2010 but also gave a further push to the theory itself. We included chapters on globalization, collective history, individual development, emotion and a diversity of practical applications. In the central chapter of the book some significant concepts were introduced like "third positions," "meta-position," "promoter position" and the most recent concept of "de-positioning." I will elaborate briefly on the last one.

The interest in de-positioning emerged from a consideration of Agnieszka who observed that studies on the dialogical self were guided by the implicit or explicit assumption that the *I* as a reflexive and dialogical agency is always bound to the flow of positions (therefore the term *I*-position). This assumption implies that the *I* is *always* a positioned *I*. In contrast to this view, she argued that the *I* is not necessarily defined by a position, but it has its own specific nature and qualities (see also Hermans-Konopka, 2012). She proposed that the *I* can become engaged in a process of *de-positioning*, implying that it has the possibility to dis-identify from any specific position and enter a form of consciousness that is discussed in the literature as witnessing, thought-free, transcendental awareness (Cahn & Polich, 2006).

During our frequent discussions about awareness, we noticed that many students seemed to confuse the process of de-positioning with the concept of meta-position. Certainly, in taking a meta-position, we see a first indication that the *I* is able to "leave" specific positions, to rise above them as if being in a helicopter, and look at them, including their interrelationships, from a certain distance. However, in taking a meta-position, one remains attached to and influenced by specific positions in the self. That is, the *I* is bound to the content of the positions and, despite some distancing, remains constrained by them. The meta-position can be influenced by a critical *I*-position (I look at the positions in my life from a critical point of view) or by an ironic *I*-position (I look at my positions in an ironic or humorous perspective). However, the de-positioning *I* is no longer attached to or influenced by any particular position but participates in a broader space of transcendental awareness which is often described in the literature as a mystical experience.

The notion of de-positioning appealed strongly to me because I remember some experiences in my life which could be described in this way. Here is one of them:

As a 15–year-old boy, I was playing together with some friends in one of the meadows between the remnants of a fortification in the neighborhood of my parents' house. At one point, I was standing there for a moment alone, with my friends at some distance. I was suddenly impressed by the enormous space above and around me. I felt a kind of intensified energy, a very vital one, a heightened awareness. I was not motivated to any action and I was not focused on any thought and did not give my attention to any specific object. I only remember that my whole environment radiated an unspeakable beauty. I felt an intense but peaceful connection with everything around me. The boundaries between the environment and myself did not disappear, but became open to an unusual degree. The experience lasted not more than one minute or so, but it remained in my memory forever. Strange enough, I did not talk about it with anybody all those years, probably because I did not know any language that could verbalize it and there was no person or group who ever invited me to talk about it. Yet, it enriched my life significantly and even now, when writing about it, I feel a kind of vibration in my body when I go back to it in my memory and imagination.[7]

When Agnieszka and I explored the literature on mystical experiences, we discovered a chapter by Foreman (1999), who describes a particular state of mind which he called a "unifying mystical experience." I see my own experience as having a striking similarity to his description (for other types of mystical experiences in the context of Dialogical Self Theory, see Hermans & Hermans-Konopka, 2010).

NOTES

1. For the combination of personal and social (including professional) positions, see Hermans & Hermans-Konopka, 2010. This combination can be seen as one of the attempts to bring society (e.g., in the form of professional positions) and the self (e.g., in the form of personal positions) together in one integrative conceptual framework. For research and discussion of the combination of personal and professional positions in an educational setting, see Leijen and Kullasepp (in press).

2. Rae Carlson, past president of the Society for Personology, invited me in 1992 to become First International Associate of this society.

3. Later I wrote with colleagues an article on the Narcissus story representing the experience of unfulfilled love, a theme closely related to the Fugit Amor experience as inspired by Dante's Divine Comedy (see Hermans, Hermans-Jansen & Van Gilst, 1991). See also Chapter 3 of the present book for a elaboration of this theme.

4. For a full description of the method and underlying theoretical principles, see Hermans & Hermans-Jansen (1995).

5. In order to introduce the other-in-the-self, I constructed a new method, the Personal Position Repertoire (PPR) method, in which internal positions (e.g., I as son of my father, I as artistic, I as ambitious) and external positions (e.g., my father, my colleague John, my opponent Theo) are brought together. Internal and external positions are combined in a matrix which allows the calculations of several indices which reflect the organization of the self-repertoire as a whole. Moreover, I experimented with dialogical relationships between positions (e.g. between I as a child and I as an autonomous person). For a full description of the method, see Hermans (2001b). Note that we also adapted the Self-Confrontation Method as informed by Dialogical Self Theory (e.g., by inviting a client to formulate personal valuations from the perspective of different I-positions with one position giving a response to the valuations of the other position (Hermans & Hermans-Jansen, 1995).

6. For a more extensive review of the origin of the dialogical self with reference to historical developments at the University of Nijmegen, see Belzen (2006).

7. For an overview of memories of mystic experiences in childhood, see Kohnstamm (2007).

Chapter Two

How an Incidental
Remark Can Change a Life

The Early Emergence of a
Promoter Position

The only normal people are the ones you don't know very well

Alfred Adler

The lowest point in my life was when I was bullied at school. Being 15 minutes at the playground, surrounded by high walls of dark stones, was a torment. As a nine-year-old boy I was standing with my back to the wall near a corner, waiting for things to come. After a few minutes, a "gang" of four to five boys approached me with balled fists and started to hit me. At that time I did not understand why this happened, but it put me "aside," somewhere in a marginalized position in my class.

Unexpectedly, another boy sometimes joined me in my shelter corner. He did not say anything to me and we never played together. We were just standing there silently, as two isolated figures, side by side, waiting for the moment that the break was over. When he was there, I was never bullied. He was one head taller than the other boys, who apparently were afraid to attack him or me. I experienced him as a kind of protecting angel. His pure presence saved me from being a powerless victim of the "plays" of my classmates and he became a kind of silent friend. Later, I realized that he was as marginal as I was: he was "too tall," I as an introverted dreamer was "too far away" to be acceptable for the group.

Not only socially, but also in learning I was decreasing. I was sitting in the classroom, but mentally I was somewhere else, making excursions and travels to all spaces in my private fantasy land. I did not hear what the teacher said and, as a result, I received low grades, particularly in arithmetic. An uncle tried to help me by giving me extra lessons in the evening. However, he used an arithmetic method that was strongly different from the one I had learned in school, so that I became even more confused than I already was. My uncle did not understand why I couldn't learn the simple tasks and, like my teacher, he was disappointed about my performance. Independently of each other, they arrived at the same conclusion: I was just "stupid." Ignorant of each other's contradicting instructions, they formed a coalition although they never met. They both let me know that they found me a "bad pupil" and that they were pessimistic about my future.

The whole situation is represented by a scene that I will remember my whole life. It is like a film fragment that has a vivid pictorial quality and an intense emotional impact at the same time. I was sitting every morning in a small room, just before going to school, having breakfast together with my uncle (who lived in our house) and my younger brothers. At some moment we heard a gradually approaching voice in the street. It was the ragman who was shouting his characteristic "Lomleeh" (a deformed pronunciation of "rags" in Dutch). As soon as my uncle heard this word, he raised his finger and with signaling eyes he said: "There is Hubert!" a ritual that was repeated a few times each week. This identification with the ragman was particularly killing for my already broken self-esteem, and I started to believe that I was indeed unable to do *anything* valuable. This growing conviction was further confirmed by my teacher at school who decided that I could not be promoted to the next grade and had to repeat the whole year.

The second year of the same grade started not very different from the first one. I continued to live in my dreaming world and the new teacher gave me a nickname "the sleeper," a name that haunted me for the rest of my primary school time. He sometimes criticized and ridiculed me in the presence of the other pupils and my self-esteem went further down. I came to the point that I experienced that I was just "nothing," "futile," a "zero." The only thing I could do is to further retreat into myself.

TURNING POINT: WHAT'S IN A MOMENT?

My new teacher was generally seen as the most strict and stern teacher of the school. He often started the lesson by taking a heavy measuring stick in his hand and giving a hard blow on the surface of the desk. His shouting "Silence!" filled the whole space and made the startled pupils afraid of making any deviation from the rules. Moreover, he disciplined the class by frequent punishments. When we were writing, he used to walk between the rows and check what was there over the shoulders of his pupils. When he noticed a mistake, he used to give a number of blows with his right hand on the back of your head, often leading to a slightly dizzy feeling and a "singing" brain.

Sometimes, this teacher went with the whole class to a place nearby the school where we could play soccer. Dressed in his long black gown with jingling garland, he joined the game. Once, just after such a match, he did something that later appeared to be a turning point in my life. He approached me, stood still for a moment, then gave me a friendly clap on my shoulder and said, "You played quite well, Hermans" (pupils were called with their surname only). This short sentence did not make a deep impression immediately. I was rather surprised as if my mind could not grasp the meaning of his utterance. Very gradually, I became aware that he said something positive about me. It must be true, since a person whom I saw as an absolute authority said it. Gradually, his words penetrated deeper into my mind and I began to realize there was "something" in which I was "good" at. His remark became written in my mind as a whitening color against a black background. It contrasted sharply with all the derogations, devaluations, and ridicules that had infiltrated my mind in the past years. Apparently, his encouragement did not function as a dramatic change at one moment. It was more like Ariadne's

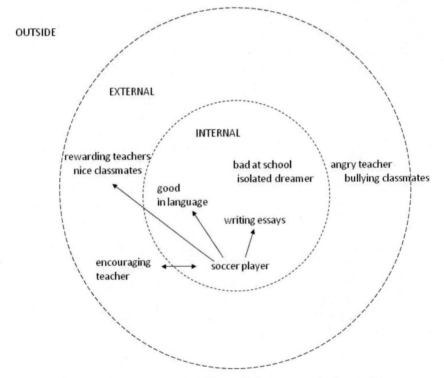

Figure 2.1.   Promoter position (soccer player) in the context of other positions.

thread that helped me to move out of a dark cage. It was a starting point of a new phase in my life. It was my "kairos," a supreme moment in which I received an unexpected gift. It gave me a sense of direction in the dark spaces of my mind. I knew where to go. I tried to further develop my soccer skills and "to play well." I started to believe that I was able to achieve *something* that came from my own capacities and, at the same time, was recognized by other people: authorities and peers.

I associate this experience with Ariadne's thread, because the simple clap on my shoulder and the confirmation it expressed was the beginning of a process that was running over many years. The skill of playing soccer which was attributed to me by a significant other and that I later attributed to myself, was gradually generalizing to other areas, even to some of the subjects taught at school. I discovered that I was good in languages and in writing essays. The result was that my teachers started to appreciate my efforts in these areas. Even my classmates, for whom physical capacities and strength were primary, started to accept me as one of them. Gradually, I found the ways to get affirmation and support from my teachers and classmates. This had important affective implications. The self-confidence and self-worth that originated from practicing soccer, generalized later to other subjects, including other forms of sport and scholastic achievements.

THE DEVELOPMENTAL
SIGNIFICANCE OF A PROMOTER POSITION

What happened to me during the process described can be illustrated by Figure 2.1. This figure draws upon an idea, already proposed by classic figures like William James and Gustav Jung, that the self can be depicted as a circle. Let's depict it as two (open) circles. The inner circle represents the internal domain of the self in which "internal self-positions" are located (e.g., I as inferior, I as an isolated dreamer) and the outer circle represents the external (extended) domain of the self in which "external self-positions" find their place (e.g., my bullying classmates, my angry teacher). Both internal and external positions belong to the self: they are experienced as "me" or "mine" and they represent transient or more permanent perspectives from which I appreciate, recognize, accept, criticize or reject myself and the world. Internal and external positions are typically, but not necessarily, "corresponding," that is, they are responding to each other in my mind. They tend to invite or evoke each other. For example, my "angry, depreciating teacher" functioned as an external position and "I as inferior" as a corresponding internal one. Likewise, my encouraging teacher was an external position and "I as a good soccer player" a corresponding internal one. Positions can be experienced as positive and pleasant (e.g. "I as good in writing essays" or "my encouraging teacher") or as negative and unpleasant ("I as inferior" or "my angry teacher"). They receive a place on the powerful positive-negative dimension that is central in the affective realms of the self.

The dynamic relationship between external and internal positions has developmental consequences. Positions can evoke each other in a particular *succession*, creating a chain: one position leads to a next one and, in its turn, this position leads again to another one. In my case there was a clear movement from my encouraging teacher who selected, confirmed, and stimulated my skills as a soccer player. From the time that the "good player" was affectively rooted in my position repertoire, I was able to evoke and develop other positions and give them a developmental impetus. When I experienced positive feelings in one position, I used this position, including its skills, capacities, motivation and emotions, to develop myself in other areas. It was even a bit more complex. There were positions that led not only to *one* next position but had the capacity to give a developmental impetus to a certain *variety* of positions simultaneously. I used the motivation that emerged from my activities as soccer player to perform well also in other areas. I wanted to develop myself as a writer of essays but also, and in the same period, to improve my language skills. Moreover, I received favorable responses from my classmates (see the arrows in Figure 2.1). Such a position that is able to open and stimulate a diversity of developmental trajectories can be qualified as a "promoter position."[1]

From Soccer Player to University Professor

In the course of my development, the position of soccer player was not a permanent one because at a certain age I simply stopped for purely physical reasons, although I did so with some regret. The position of the "good soccer player," and its motivational and emotional significance, was more a developmental impetus than a fixed and stable element in my repertoire. In its generalizing potential it produced, during my life-course, a broader range of positions that became even more influential than its origin. The most significant position that emerged from it was "I as ambitious." This position was clearly more general than the more specific "soccer player" because it applied to a broader variety of situations, in my past, present, and future. Moreover, this position worked not simply in its isolation. It was able to form a coalition with some other positions that emerged in different periods of my life, but had in common that they went into the same developmental direction. As the oldest son of my parents, I wanted them to be proud of me and of my performance at school.

Later, as a university student I wanted to achieve high grades and wanted to be as free as possible to achieve my personal purposes. As a dissertation student I was motivated to create something new and influential. As the subject of my dissertation, I chose to study achievement motivation and fear of failure. These concepts formed the basis of two psychological tests that were new in my country, one for adults and one for children.

I'm sharing these professional events in order to show that much of this work was associated, and even fed by, my ambitious position. There was always this drive to go on, to perform better, to create new things, to improve myself, and to make something that was valuable for science and society. It was a *contribution* but, from the perspective of my ambitious position, it was *my* contribution. At the same time, it is very clear that this position, although I'm becoming increasingly critical about its shadow sides, has brought me much value in my life. It helped me to finish my studies, to work on a dissertation which I completed within two and half a years, to become a professor at a young age, to make travels to different countries and cultures, and to meet many people and colleagues in the international scene whom I would never have met without the driving force of my ambitious position.

However, the gradual change from a social outcast to an appreciated soccer player and, later, to a recognized social scientist, cannot simply be depicted as a linear movement from point A to point B. Such a movement would suggest that the more I reach point B, the farther I'm removed from point A. In contradiction to such a view, the dark side of myself, the inferior position, stayed always at the background and could become foreground in situations that look innocent or neutral at first sight. It could popup at unexpected moments and cause embarrassing situations. Around 50 years after my primary school time, I was at a camping site where the manager, in the presence of apparently amused others, playfully ridiculed my driving behavior. This simple event disorganized and confused me for some hours. I was surprised that such a simple event could have such a strong impact on my feelings (of shame and inferiority). Somewhere, the camping owner was in my experience "functionally equivalent" to the "angry and devaluating teachers" in myself and the campers to my early classmates. Similar emotions were evoked in both situations.

The inferior position, waiting behind the scenes in order to suddenly take the central place of the platform, sometimes made me feel useless, valueless, and insignificant in the eyes of others and myself. This occurred even "silently" during meetings at the university that often made me feel tense and closed. When I was there, I found that the other participants had meaningful things to say about a diversity of subjects, like the acquisitions of grants, the reconstruction of the curriculum, or the installment of a new committee. During such meetings, I was typically silent because I did not have the feeling that

I had something significant to say. It was my feeling that the others had much more valuable ideas to contribute and, therefore, I simply shut my mouth. This resulted, however, in an increasing tension in me, originating, as I discovered later, from my earlier position as a social outcast. This tension was the reason that I was actually often absent from such meetings.

As the preceding description suggests, I discovered that my ambitious position was not something that can be considered in itself. Apparently, it originated from the inferior position and helped to keep it under control and to compensate for it by performing well in science, teaching, sport, piano playing, and discussions with colleagues. These aspects of my development can be well understood from an Adlerian perspective that makes us under-stand that an early experience of inferiority functions as a motivational source for a later striving for perfection and superiority. When I look at my develop-ment from the perspective of Dialogical Self Theory, I see a basic conflict between two powerful *I*-positions, the inferior and the ambitious. In my early school years, the former was overwhelmingly present and, as associated with intensely negative emotions, functioned as a fertile source for the emergence of the latter.

Although the ambitious became, particularly in my early and middle adult-hood, a source of pleasure and pride, and even became a motivational force in itself, it simultaneously had the function of an emotionally driven counter-position to the inferior. As such it had to keep the self as a whole in a state of balance and able to cope with situations that implied a possible threat to my self-worth and self-esteem. The nature of the field of tension between the two positions needs some further exploration. The always existing possibility that the inferior could "take the power" in the self, requires a discussion of a special phenomenon, described as "coalition of positions."

THE STRENGTH OF A COALITION IN THE SELF

As described, my ambitious position became, in the course of time, more and more dominant over the inferior because it was sustained by some other posi-tions that were present early in my life. As a promoter position, the ambitious received support from positions that were already central in the lives of my parents. My father could be described as a hard worker in an independent business and as a warm Burgundian character at the same time. As a baker he rose at 4.00 AM in order to bake breads and pies for his customers. At the end of the afternoon he used to go to a café in the neighborhood where he played billiards and had fun with friends. His three positions, the hard worker, the free entrepreneur, and the enjoyer of life, were not separated positions. He could combine them easily and naturally. He used to work and had great pleasure in selling "sweet things." In my imagination, I see him, with a mild

EXERCISE 2.1

The following exercise might be helpful when you want to compare several important *I*-positions and their development. The purpose of this exercise is to discover possible tensions between the development of these positions and to explore what is your answer to these tensions.

Here is the starting question. Are there positions in your life that are important to you and in which you have the feeling that you are making progress? Please select three positions from your life and formulate them in your own words. They can be social positions (e.g., I as a professional, I as a father or mother, husband or wife, I as a leader, I as a colleague or any other) or personal ones (e.g., I as ambitious, I as jealous, I as a pessimist, I as a music lover, or any other). Select also three positions in your life in which you have the feeling that you are making regress. Choose your *own* positions in your *own* formulations.

Positions in which I feel *progress*:
Position 1: "I as _____ "
Position 2: "I as _____ "
Position 3: "I as _____ "

Positions in which I feel *regress*:
Position 4: "I as _____ "
Position 5: "I as _____ "
Position 6: "I as _____ "

Now concentrate on the question: To what extent do you feel these positions are *important for your life-fulfillment.*

Position 1:
unimportant—rather important—important—very important
to my life-fulfillment.

Position 2:
unimportant—rather important—important—very important
to my life-fulfillment.

Position 3:
unimportant—rather important—important—very important
to my life-fulfillment

Position 4:
unimportant—rather important—important—very important

Position 5:
unimportant—rather important—important—very important

Position 6:
unimportant—rather important—important—very important

Question 1
Are there any of the mentioned positions that are important or very important to your life-fulfillment but in which you have the feeling that you are making regress? In that case you notice a discrepancy between 'importance' and 'fulfillment.' In which position(s) do you notice such a discrepancy?

_____

_____

_____

EXERCISE 2.1 (*Continued*)

Question 2
If you notice a discrepancy in one or more positions,
what do you see as the origin of the discrepancy? When did it start?

_____

_____

_____

Question 3
What is your answer to this discrepancy now?

_____

_____

_____

smile on his face entering the bakery shop with a basket in his hands, filled with warm, pleasantly smelling bread, "fresh from the oven." I recognize this combination of work, freedom and pleasure in my own life which assist in my being able to work many hours without any fatigue. I have the feeling that intellectual work gives me energy rather than deplete me. The work as a university professor, moreover, gave me a considerable freedom to follow my own interests and to ´bake´ something made by myself. I was permitted to choose my own research subject and to teach those subjects that emanated from literature that inspired me. Moreover, the university allowed me to work part-time at home where I could work as a co-therapist together with my first wife, Els Hermans-Jansen, in her independent practice. In my view, this combination of "I as ambitious," "I as enjoyer of life," and "I as a freedom seeker," went well together to do the work as a scientist and practitioner. The coalition of these three significant positions enabled me to cope with the monster of inferiority and futility that had so darkly colored the early years of my primary school period. At the same time, I'm aware of the fact that the inferior still exists in the background of myself and can become prominent at moments in which I am exposed to events or persons that specifically appeal to this position.

The fact that the inferiority position was associated with very negative (unpleasant) emotions does not mean that this position is "useless" or "meaningless" from a developmental point of view. First of all, it gave a strong impetus to the emergence of other positions that became, finally, an end in themselves, loaded as they were with pleasure and a sense of meaning. Second, I know what it is to "bite the dust" and to be a social outcast. I can easily identify with any person who is qualified, by others or themselves, as a "loser," a "nitwit," or a "persona non-grata." Similarly, experiences of people who are discriminated on the basis of their race, religion, age or sex are familiar for me, although formally I don't formally belong to any of the inferior categories (with the exception of my age). Third, I discovered that experiences that are negative in the beginning can become positive as parts of an autobiographical memory. The bullying by my classmates and the frequent physical punishments by my teachers are felt as contributions to my development and as making me the person I'm now. From my *present* perspective, I experience these events, emotionally, as more positive than negative. With nostalgia I think back at that period in my life as an adventure. I would like to go back, at least for a short period of time, to experience it again as a contrast to my present life. For sure, one event will always stay in my mind as a milestone: the clap on my shoulder by my teacher of the third grade. I never met him again and could not find him when I searched for him. I could not tell him that his "small encouragement" given at the "right moment" was for me an event with far reaching consequences. Probably, he would not remember it. Teachers are often involuntarily ignorant of the dramatic impact that small remarks or gestures can have for the rest of the lives of their pupils.

During the writing of this book, I went back to the monastery where he was working as a teacher for many years, because I felt a strong wish to thank him for the significant role he played in my life. There I heard that he had left the monastery many years ago, married an African woman, and died in Sierra Leone in 1966 at a young age. While he was such a vivid memory for me during all those years, it was shock to hear that he passed away such a long time ago.

THE TRANSFORMATION OF AN
ORIGINAL NEGATIVE EXPERIENCE

Although the inferior was, as it seems to be, effectively counter-acted by the ambitious over the years, it never disappeared from the scene entirely. Rather, he was energizing me to develop myself into an opposite direction, that is, from an inferior to the (superior) ambitious position. Gradually, the ambitious one became stronger and developed to such a degree that I was able to

EXERCISE 2.2
Here is an exercise which refers to the existence of a promoter position in your life.

Question 1
Do you consider one of the positions mentioned in the previous exercise as a *promoter position*? Which one?

_____

_____

_____

Question 2
Had this position already a promoter function in the past and does it still have this function in the present?

_____

_____

_____

Question 3
Are there any (opposite) positions to which the promoter position reacts?

_____

_____

_____

Question 4
When you look at your positions mentioned in this exercise, is there any external promoter position (a significant other) that played or is still playing a significant role in your development (e.g. a friend, teacher, husband, wife, parent, colleague, or a person or being who is prominent in your imagination)? Can you pose a question to him or her in your imagination?

_____

_____

_____

What is his or her imagined answer?

_____

_____

_____

push the inferior to the background. By the distance in time and building up a career, the inferior gradually lost its overwhelming and threatening character. Little by little, and sometimes with considerable fluctuations, the ambitious became strong enough to keep the inferior and associated emotions under control. The struggle between my both sides, the ambitious and the inferior, as I look back at it, did not resemble a dialogical relation. The ambitious was not willing to listen in any way to the inferior, but just wanted to compensate for it, by getting high grades, by trying to gain recognition and admiration from teachers and co-students and by being competitive by trying to perform better than others. This external orientation had a clearly internal correlation: as an achiever I was fighting, persistently, against my threatening internal opponent, the inferior. Between these adversaries there was no dialogue at all. Instead, there were two *successive monologues.* Initially, the inferior occupied the centre of the stage, believing that there could be no more than failure and futility from my side. In performance situations there was no other position that could compensate for that. Later, when the ambitious emerged, I invested all my effort in kicking the inferior off the stage, not willing to entertain any meaningful relationship with this "untouchable." Rather than understanding the inferior, the ambitious wanted to simply push him to the background. In the long run, this looked like a successful operation, particularly in my early and middle adulthood. Affirmed by the positive feedback from evaluation committees and peer-reviews, the ambitious, in coalition with the freedom seeker, could further tighten his grip on the inferior who was further marginalized as an unwanted figure in myself.

The one-sided fight for dominance in the self, however, showed a transformation after I became an emeritus professor. In this period I arrived in a situation in which I could, more freely than before, devote much of my time to writing, reading, and creating methods for assessing and developing of the dialogical self. Moreover, I contributed as a teacher and trainer to a post-graduate training course on the Self-Confrontation Method. A further turning point in my life was my meeting Agnieszka Konopka at one of the International Conferences on the Dialogical Self. I fell in love with her and this finally led to the divorce from my first wife. From that time on, we have cooperated together on the further development of Dialogical Self Theory and developed methods for its assessment and stimulation. During our many discussions, we looked, more carefully than before, at our lives and found out that the theory was helpful in understanding and articulating some significant developments in our selves. One of the discoveries was that I could, more often than before, smile *about* and even *at* the "small boy" so that he had the guts to come out of his dark corner and show his face. Gradually, the inferior became a more accepted part of myself and I experienced a better relationship with it than ever. He was no longer the same as the one to whom I was subjected at a younger age. Rather than pushing the inferior to the background, I started to look at him and give him more attention. I began to realize that he was a part of myself that I could not simply delete and also that it did not make much sense to be continuously involved in an endless struggle with it. This came to a point that I discovered there was some value in this dark figure. I learned to make a productive use of the inferior in coping with difficult situations. When I felt "insulted" by people whom I saw as "overly critical" or as "unfair," I trained myself to stop responding with counter-criticism or anger, although that was often my first "instinctive" reaction." Instead, I learned to move into a *different* position, one that was *not* located on the dimension attack vs. defense. When I received a response that could be easily interpreted as an attack, insult or ridicule, I succeeded to give a response that was different from the ones to which I was programmed by my early personal experiences (retreating in myself) and by my evolutionary history (fight-flight). For example, when I was, in my view, unfairly tackled by opponents, I could ask myself the question "What can I learn from this?" In this context, I could be amused by a philosopher who once said you can learn more from your enemies than from your friends. While the ambitious has been always the apparent *adversary* of the inferior who had to be beaten at all costs, the "learner" gave the inferior, as part of a process of transformation, *more space* to be part of myself. I'm now in a period of my life that, in cases of disapproval or denigration, I can say to myself: "Okay, this is a bit painful, but let's make something of it." I do not suppress the inferior and I don't try to push him away from the scene with force. I can be angry when I feel attacked or unfairly criticized, and I can tolerate the presence of the emotion, but I find myself, more than before, able to *not* follow its action tendencies. That is, I experience the emotion, give it space, but do not necessarily act in the line of my first impulse. Rather than escaping from it, I go *into* it and can also *leave* it in order to move into a different direction. I find it gratifying to learn something from the experience and to take it up as part of a creative process, in which I get involved alone or together with others. Certainly, the original emotion (e.g., inferiority or anger) energizes me to do something, but what I do, is part of a larger space in which I feel the freedom to position myself in a way that I see as more productive and constructive for the self as a whole.

I noticed that the position of "learner" became finally even a kind of new promoter position that I felt as particularly enriching because it helped me to make use of my sensitivities, to get in touch with new, interesting people and to find new sources of knowledge and satisfaction. When I look at the whole process from a meta-position, the initial experience of being an "inferior" and a "failure" stimulated, finally, my curiosity and tendency to explore new situations. Being retired but still active as a scientist, I'm becoming aware of the increasing limitations of my ambitious *I*-position in a phase of my life in which I'm no longer in need of making a career. Moreover, given my age, I'm facing an increasingly limited time perspective so that I'm sure that I will never be able to realize the extreme pretensions of my ambitious position, "unrealistic" as they are considered from my present perspective.

From my ambitious position I'm fighting a lost battle. In the present phase, the learner seems to be a good "successor" of the ambitious from which he finally emerged. The learner can even create, sometimes, a productive coalition with the inferior, particularly at moments that the inferior stimulates me to take into account the multiplicity of dark and bright feelings of myself and of others. So, I feel sympathy with August Wilson, a playwright interested in the "American-African experience," who once said: "Your willingness to wrestle with your demons will cause your angels to sing. Use the pain as fuel, as a reminder of your strength."

In my early life, the inferior was the "big demon," the Minotaurus who was producing his frightening sounds from the darker spaces of the labyrinth of myself. I found out that I could not avoid this demon but had to enter into a fight with him. Finally, via the efforts of the ambitious and its transformation, I was able to enter wider and brighter spaces where I found more freedom, learning possibilities, and social rewards than before. The development to a "higher level of integration" brought me to the conclusion that there are two very different kinds of strengths. One kind is the opposite of weakness. When you are strong, you are not weak. *Instead* of feeling weak, you want to feel strong. In this conception, strong and weak are mutually exclusive and they are part of the pervasive good-bad dichotomy. Another kind of strength is when you are skilled enough to experience your weakness as an accepted or even valuable part of your experiences, able to give it space, and able to enter this experience *and* leave it without being fully determined by its action tendencies. This latter form of strength includes and tolerates the experience of weakness, as a source of energy that has the potential to open spaces where angels have the freedom to sing.

NOTE

1. From a semiotic point of view, Valsiner (2003) introduced the notion of "promoter sign." Expanding on his insights we proposed, from a dialogical perspective, the concept of "promoter position" (Hermans & Hermans-Konopka, 2010).

Chapter Three

Paradise Lost and the Imperfection of Being

> When you dream, you dialogue with aspects of yourself that normally are not with you in the daytime and you discover that you know a great deal more than you thought you did.
>
> *Toni Cade Bambara*

Almost 35 years ago, I started to describe, in a special notebook, my dreams. Not the many dreams that were coming and going every night and which one tends to forget very quickly, but those I felt as compelling, intriguing or as having a special meaning or significance. The most interesting dreams were those that asked for my special attention and gave me the feeling that they had something important to tell me. As if they had a message to which I was invited to "listen," irrespective of being able or not to grasp explicitly their meaning or message. There was one particular dream that, over the whole period of report, appeared in my mind more than a hundred times, as far as I could count them. It had the following story line:

I was walking and playing around in the garden around my house together with friends and loved ones and everything was quiet and peaceful. Surrounded by blossoming flowers and protected by the full green of the trees at the border of the forest, we felt like children playing in a miracle garden. There was no verbal interaction, no purpose, no action. It was more like a state of *being*, an intensified experience of belonging to nature and to each other.

In the second part of the dream, for reasons that never became clear, I decided to sell the house and garden. I only know that this was a decision that resulted from a preceding process of reasoning and calculation. Apparently, economical and financial arguments led me to take the decision that seemed, at that moment, entirely reasonable and clear. I had no doubt about my plan and I was convinced that it was a well-argued decision. It seemed that in this part of the dream I acted as a rational calculator.

In the third part of the dream, I found myself in another place, in a house somewhere in a dull and desolate part of a city. The house was small and had no garden. Outside there were only grey houses of cold-looking stones. The rooms of my house were empty, and the whole construction was based on straight lines. There was nothing unexpected and everything was colorless. The whole environment seemed to be constructed in the service of minimal and practical utility. There were also no people around. I was totally alone and felt alienated from myself. Feeling imprisoned in this miserable environment, I became overwhelmed by remorse that penetrated my mind as if the poisoning point of a sharp spear was going in deeper and deeper. In this painful state, I felt an intense longing to go back to my original place of life and love, but I realized that this was totally impossible. Could I buy the house back, so that I could return? No, there was not a chance! The people who bought the house and were happily living there, were much younger than I was and they would stay there even after my death. This was most painful: the combination of intense longing to return to a lost precious place and the full awareness that any return was made totally impossible as a result of my own rational but faulty decision.

This dream occurred to me over the years in many versions, as "variations on a theme." However, the basic structure was remarkably constant. The dream consisted always of three parts: the blissful experience of harmonious connection with nature and people; then the rational decision to sell the place; and then feeling panic-stricken after the discovery of being dislocated and the remorseful awareness of definite loss. The three parts in the dream were always sharply distinguished and felt like opposites: my cool and rational decision to sell my precious house contrasted strongly with the warm connection with nature and people in the first part; and the experience of desperate longing of the third part showed a stark contrast with both the experience of heavenly harmony of the first part and the cold rationality of the second one.

Although the dream, and its frequency, made me even more attached to the house than ever, something happened that was entirely beyond my expectations. I met Agnieszka Konopka at one of the International Conferences on the Dialogical Self and married her a few years later. My relationship with her led me to actually decide to sell the house, with the intention to build up a new life somewhere else. After finding an attractive location in the southern part of the Netherlands, I was in a situation in which I could see the difference between the feelings which I had after selling the house in my dream and my feelings after *actually* selling it. Somewhat to my relief, I have never regretted my decision to give up my previous place. I was and still am just glad to live in a smaller house that receives light, in every corner, from the green environment. I gives me everyday the feeling that I'm participating in a larger, open space, despite its smaller size. Apparently, the emotions that I had in my dream never came to me during my waking life after moving to the other location. Actually, I live there happily together with my new wife and never felt any regret about the house which I gave up. What could be the meaning of this dream, taking into account that my desire was, as it seemed, different from just being attached to a particular location?

RODIN'S COMPOSITION OF *FUGIT AMOR* AND THE EXPERIENCE OF UNFULFILLED LONGING

During my explorations around the dream, I realized that the theme of lost unity is a central theme in the myths of religious traditions. A very prominent version is the theme of the lost paradise, in which Adam and Eve are expelled from the Garden of Eden, after their temptation by the fallen angel Satan, as poetically depicted in the classic work *Paradise Lost* by the 17th century writer John Milton. A central turning point in this myth is the moment that Adam and Eve were eating from the Tree of Knowledge that resulted in the irreversible loss of a blissful, heavenly state of harmony and the exile to an earthy state of struggle and separation.

The themes of lost harmony and lost or broken love are not only found in the myths of religious traditions, but also in many artistic works. Once, when I visited Paris, I discovered in *Le Musée Rodin*, an artistic creation that struck me by its expressive power. It was called *Fugit Amor*, a work that was inspired by the tragic love story of Paulo and Francesca. The context of their love affair was a long-lasting conflict between Francesca's father, Guido, and Paulo's father, Malatesta. After a long conflict, the two families made peace by arranging a marriage between Guido's beautiful young daughter Francesca and Gianciotto, the eldest son of Malatesta. However, Gianciotto was ugly and deformed and therefore Guido's friends said to him that if Francesca would see him before the marriage, she would never agree with the arrangement. Therefore, they sent Gianciotto's younger brother Paolo, a handsome, pleasing, and very courteous man, to Ravenna with a full mandate to marry Francesca in Gianciotto's name. When she saw Paolo, she immediately fell in love with him. Although Francesca realized, after the deceptive marriage contract was made, that she had been deceived, the feelings of Paolo and Francesca for each other were so strong that they continued to be engaged in their forbidden love affair. Once, when Gianciotto went off on business, they became intimate. However, Gianciotto's servant discovered them and told his master all what he saw. Informed of this liaison, Gianciotto one day caught them together in Francesca's bedroom. Unaware that Paolo got stuck in his attempt to escape down a ladder, she let Gianciotto in the room. When Gianciotto lunged at Paolo with a sword, Francesca stepped between them and was killed instead. In his rage, Gianciotto then killed Paolo as well.

I found out that Rodin, in many of his works, was inspired by Dante Alighieri (1265–1321), who gave Paolo and Franscesca's tragic love affair a prominent place in his monumental work *La Divina Commedia*. Although Dante could easily identify with the lovers and was deeply moved by their story, their engagement in a forbidden love affair was enough reason for the moralistic poet to damn them to hell. They were punished to be forever in each other's immediate neighborhood, driven by an intense longing, while at the same time not being able to touch each other. As a punishment, the lovers were blown by a permanent whirlwind into an immense space, being in close proximity, at the same time being separated for eternity. A never-ending fire of love, a total absence of hope—indeed, a terrible punishment!

Impressed by Dante's moving depiction of the love story, the French artist August Rodin created a statue in which Paolo, in a backward position, stretches his arms in an attempt to embrace Francesca who is turned away from him. However, the lovers are not able to unite, but instead they are tormented by an enduring "almost touching." Interestingly enough, Rodin used the same statue of Paolo, in another context, to represent the biblical figure of the Prodigal Son. Although the same statue was used for both compositions, the difference is that in the latter case the statue is placed in an upright position. The figure stretches his arms upward and seems to be driven by an intense longing for contact with a supernatural being.

As Schmoll (1978) suggests, various compositions of Rodin, like Paolo and Francesca, the Prodigal Son, Orpheus, and other works, represent a basic theme in his oeuvre that can be summarized in terms of unfulfilled longing. Although many of his figures already appeared in older classic works, like Dante's *Divina Commedia*, the Bible, and Greek mythology, they are, as symbols of unfulfilled longing, increasingly intriguing and relevant in a modern era, ruled by an ideology of self-contained individualism. At this point, I often refer to an article by Edward Sampson (1985) who argued that the modern self has three features: sharp boundaries between self and non-self; the other is not part of the self but is seen as purely "outside"; and the relationship between self and environment is one of control. In my view, Rodin's work is particularly relevant as showing the need to escape from an isolated existence of autonomy and to (re)unite with some external being. His figures do not seem to participate in any formalized religious institution, but they are driven by an intense longing to reunite with a source from which they became increasingly isolated. The arms stretched in vain to reach some outside real or imagined figure symbolize very well the unfulfilled longing of individuals who try to get in touch with a reality (another person or a source of meaning) that has become unreachable.

WHAT DOES A *FUGIT AMOR* EXPERIENCE LOOK LIKE IN THE LIVES OF ORDINARY PEOPLE?

Impressed by the abundant presence of the *Fugit Amor* theme in mythology and art, I became curious about its affective meaning in the lives of ordinary people. Therefore, I asked five students, who did not know the story behind the statue, to identify with the position of Paolo and to express Paolo's feelings in the form of an affective profile.[1] I provided the students with a list of affect terms and asked them to assess Paolo's experience by estimating the intensity of his feelings. The results showed that the students agreed that Paolo's experience could be characterized by a high intensity of affect referring to the longing for contact and union with the other: love, tenderness, caring, and intimacy. At the same time, some negative feelings were part of this experience: powerlessness, loneliness, worry, and unhappiness. The feeling with the highest intensity level was love, in combination with high levels of powerlessness. On the basis of these results, I concluded that Paolo's position in relation to Francesca, as expressed in Rodin's statue, could be described as an experience of unfulfilled longing for a loved, but at the same time, unreachable other.

Narcissus Stretching His Hands Out to the Water

The *Fugit Amor* theme aroused my vivid interest, as it was linked to my training (in the fifties of the previous century) in a kind of high school known as the *Gymnasium*, that had a curriculum heavily loaded with languages. The program was obligatory and contained 6 languages at that time: 3 hours per week of English, 3 hours of French, 3 hours of German, 3 hours of Dutch, 6 hours of Latin and 6 hours of Greek, with the striking absence of anything about economy or finances. Over the years (6 in total) we devoted an enormous amount of time to the translation of Greek and Latin texts which were seen, with reverence, as representing the origin of our Western civilization. One of them who had a central place in the translation program was Ovid, who became most famous for his poetic *Metamorphoses*. Only more than 40 years later, when I became involved in the multi-voiced nature of the self, did

I become aware of linkages between the concept of metamorphosis and the multiplicity of the self.

I became particularly interested of one of Ovid's greatest stories, the Narcissus myth, with its central part: Narcissus looking into the water.[2] In order to understand the context of this part, I present a summary of the Roman version of the myth, as narrated in Ovid's *Metamorphoses*:

> Echo, a nymph, falls in love with a youth named Narcissus, who was the son of the blue Nymph Liriope of Thespia. The river god Cephisus had once encircled Liriope with the windings of his streams, and thus trapping her, had seduced the nymph who gave birth to an exceptionally beautiful boy. Concerned about the welfare of such a beautiful child, Liriope consulted the prophet Tiresias regarding her son's future. Tiresias told the nymph that Narcissus would live to a ripe old age, "if he didn't come to know himself." When he had reached "his sixteenth year"... every youth and girl in the town was in love with him, but he haughtily spurned them all.
>
> One day when Narcissus was out hunting stags, Echo stealthily followed the handsome youth through the woods, longing to address him but unable to speak first. When Narcissus finally heard footsteps and shouted "Who's there?" Echo answered "Who's there?" So it went, until finally Echo showed herself and rushed to embrace the lovely youth. He pulled away from the nymph and vainly told her to leave him alone. Narcissus left Echo heartbroken and she spent the rest of her life in lonely glens, pining away for the love she never knew, until only her voice remained.
>
> Not all the lovers of Narcissus were so passive. One of them took his complaint about rejection to the goddess of vengeance, Nemesis. The rejected suitor asked the goddess Nemesis to make Narcissus fall in love with himself, but simultaneously to be incapable of accepting his own love.
>
> Nemesis heard this prayer and sent Narcissus his punishment. He came across a deep pool in a forest, from which he took a drink. As he did, he saw his reflection for the first time in his life and fell in love with the beautiful boy he was looking at, not realizing that he was looking at himself. Eventually, after pining away for a while, he realized that the image he saw in the pool was actually a reflection of himself. Realizing that he could not act upon this love, he tore at his dress and beat at his body, his life force draining out of him. As he died, the bodiless Echo came upon him and felt sorrow and pity. His soul was sent to "the darkest hell" and the narcissus flower grew where he died. It is said that Narcissus still keeps gazing on his image in the waters of the river Styx.

In an empirical study on this myth, in collaboration with Els Hermans-Jansen and Willem van Gilst, we focused on its central part: Narcissus looking into the water and falling in love with his mirror image. Like in the case of Rodin's statue, we invited some students to identify with the position of Narcissus as trying to touch the image in vain and to assess the experience of

Narcissus at that moment. We found again that the students agreed with each other about the nature of the affective experience. It was characterized by high levels of love, tenderness, caring and intimacy, in combination with high levels of powerlessness, loneliness, worry, and unhappiness. We concluded that the experience of Narcissus, although on a manifest level quite different than the story of Paolo and Francesca, had on a deeper level the same affective meaning: the experience of unfulfilled longing for another (or another in the self) who is or has become unreachable.

When we compared the experience of Narcissus with the feelings clients reported in relation to important events in their own lives, we found that they referred to some social or existential shortcomings. Here are some typical examples of events formulated by clients in their own words:

- I think it is too bad that I couldn't remove some of my mother's loneliness with my cheerfulness when she was still alive.
- First, I meant everything to him. Now he means everything to me. The roles are now reversed.
- I would like to share things in an equal, friendly way with my father but we both avoid it; we both hang on to our roles as father and child.
- Dick's suicide: failing to do anything for him; not being able to stop him; that I didn't see through it all.
- I think it is terrible that my sister and I can't communicate sensitively.

Studying experiences of this type and comparing them with the affective connotation of the *Fugit Amor* experience, I realized that in their content (the texts formulated by the clients) were reflections of a common theme. They referred to a basic human experience, the unfulfilled longing towards a loved, but unreachable, other. This conclusion made me think of the difference between the story of Narcissus and the psychological notion of narcissism. I realized that they are more different than one would expect on the basis of the similarity of the words. While *narcissism*, from a Freudian perspective, is seen as an aberration resulting from an investment of libido in one's own self at the cost of investing it in others, the *Narcissus story* reflects a basic longing for union with another person (or something or someone in one's self) who is or has become unreachable.

The questionable association of the Narcissus story with the phenomenon of narcissism and the dysfunction Narcissistic personality disorder may have well contributed to the pejorative perception of the figure of Narcissus involved as he is in his self-image. From our studies of the affective properties of the *Fugit Amor* and Narcissus experience, I have learned that these experiences are entirely different or even opposed to the connotations of the phenomenon of narcissism and narcissistic personality disorder.

The central point I want to make is this. There seems to be a commonality on a deeper level among the position of Paolo in Rodin's composition, stretching out his hands in vain to reach Francesca, the position of the prodigal son stretching his hand, in a moment of desperation, towards an invisible power above him, and Narcissus reaching in vain for the image of another or (later) himself. In these artistic works, the stretching hands that will never reach their goal symbolize a deeper existential experience that, in my view, can be understood in terms of Lacan's (1966) notion of *Le manque d'etre* (the lack of being). This is not a shortcoming in the sense of a need for a specific object or person that can be fulfilled by possessing this object or reaching this person. Rather, the being itself is a shortcoming. In my understanding of this deficiency, a person is, metaphorically speaking, not complete but rather "half a person." Given this basic state of deficiency, the person is not incidentally, but on a more fundamental level, desiring another state of existence or longing for another person or being from which one feels separated in order to find a complement of himself. In its existential meaning, this deficiency is broader and more fundamental than the experience of not being able to reach a loved one. It refers to the human condition as an imperfect state of existence.

THE DUALITY OF MOTIVATION

Stimulated by my own dreams, the stories of participants in my research and discussions with clients in psychotherapy, I became more and more interested in what can be described as the duality of human motivation. The basic idea is that the person on the one hand is an autonomous entity that attempts to maintain and enhance itself as an independent being, and on the other hand part of some larger whole that transcends this separate and autonomous existence. This duality is, under different labels, pervasively present in the psychological literature. Angyal (1966), both a system theorist and a self-theorist, assumed two directional trends which he called autonomy (or self-determination) and homonomy (or self-surrender). The trend toward autonomy aims at expansion of the self by assimilating and mastering the environment, as expressed in the striving for exploration, acquisition, achievement and superiority. The trend toward homonomy motivates people to fit themselves with their environment and to participate in some larger whole. Homonomy becomes manifest in finding a harmonious connection with a social group, with nature, or with a supernatural being. It is expressed in love, harmony in social relations, aesthetic experiences, and in the connection with nature.

In my lectures about the duality thesis, I used to refer to Angyal who characterized the paradoxical nature of a human being by defining him, in a most succinct way, as a "part-whole," that is, being autonomous as a *whole* but homonymous as a *part* of some larger context. He proposed that for psychological health the realization of both trends are necessary.

In my further explorations of the literature, I found out that the distinction between autonomy and homonymy is strikingly similar to Bakan's (1966) well-known distinction between agency (self-assertion and self-expansion) and communion (being at one with other organisms). For understanding the relationship between agency and communion in the context of the modern self, Bakan's notion of "unmitigated agency" is particularly relevant: "One of the fundamental points which I attempt to make is that the very split of agency from communion, which is a separation, arises from the agency feature itself and it represses the communion from which it has separated itself" (pp. 14–15). In the modern self, as influenced by the Enlightenment and protestant ethic, he observes forms of "unmitigated agency," amongst others, in the prevalence of activity over receptivity, the importance of saving and making profit, and the emphasis on self-control. This exaggeration is accompanied by the neglect or even distrust against "Gemütlichkeit" (coziness) and emotions.[3]

Many years after I was reading about the phenomenon of "unmitigated agency," I travelled through South Africa in May 2011. One of the universities where I lectured at was the University of Kwazulu-Natal, where several dissertation students, both black and white, were applying Dialogical Self Theory to different topics. One of the topics was the phenomenon of "hegemonic masculinity" that shows a striking similarity to the concept of unmitigated agency. It refers to cultural power relations in which the maintenance of idealized dominant masculinity is encouraged. Among its defining characteristics are emotional control, autonomy, risk taking, competitiveness, aggression, power over women, and homophobia (Kahn, Holmes, & Brett, 2011). Some of the students were doing research on the relationship between masculinity and rape and they told me that their interest was stimulated by findings that South Africa has some of the highest incidents of rape, including child and baby rape. I was shocked to see the excessively high rates and the powerful role of cultural factors that facilitated it. In a survey among 1,500 schoolchildren in the Soweto township, for example, it was found that a quarter of all the boys said that "jackrolling," a term used for "gang rape," was fun.

THE CIRCLE OF POSITIONS AS ROOTED IN BASIC MOTIVES

Over the years we applied the Self-Confrontation Method in our psychotherapeutic practice and collected material from many hundreds of clients of different socio-economic and educational levels (Hermans & Hermans-Jansen, 1995). It gave us a chance to study the affective properties of these experiences in referring to the basic motives of self-enhancement and contact with the other. This resulted in six main types of experiences that could be depicted in a circle in which the tree axes represent opposite types (see Figure 3.1). Each type of experience is associated with a typical narrative theme. For example, when we found a combination of a high level of affect referring to self-enhancement (e.g. pride and self-confidence) and a high level of general-positive affect (e.g. happiness and enjoyment) (so-called +S experience), we noticed in the formulation of these experiences by our clients a narrative theme typically referring to autonomy or success. Or, when we found high levels of affect referring to contact and union (e.g. love and tenderness) together with a high level of general-negative feelings (e.g. unhappiness and disappointment) (so-called -O experience), then the formulations of these valuations typically referred to the theme of unfulfilled love (see the *Fugit Amor* and the Narcissus experience as discussed earlier in the present chapter).[4] The types of experience as depicted in the circle correspond with *I*-positions in a multi-voiced dialogical self and can be summarized in this way:

- I as successful or I as an autonomous person (+S), associated with a high level of affect referring to self-assertion and, at the same time, with many positive feelings. This position is typical of a strong orientation to work, career, achievement, competition, and social power.
- I as angry or I as opposed (-S), associated with a high level of affect referring to self-assertion and, at the same time, with many negative feelings. This combination of affect is often found in forms of protest, aggression, hate, and revenge.
- I as a loving or I as connected (+O), associated with a high level of affect referring to contact and, at the same time, with many positive feelings. This union combination of affect is expressed in receptivity and openness toward another person, to art or spirituality. We find it also in intimate forms of sexual contact.
- I as mourning or I as desperately longing (-O), associated with a high level of affect referring to contact and union and, at the same time, with many negative feelings. We find this experience in situations of loss of a significant other, in tragic love, broken relationships, and unfulfilled desire.
- I as imprisoned or I as powerless and isolated (-LL), associated with a low level of affect referring to self-assertion, a low level of affect referring to contact and union and, at the same time, many negative feelings. This experience is typical of victimization, trauma, some forms of depression, and feeling locked up in oneself.

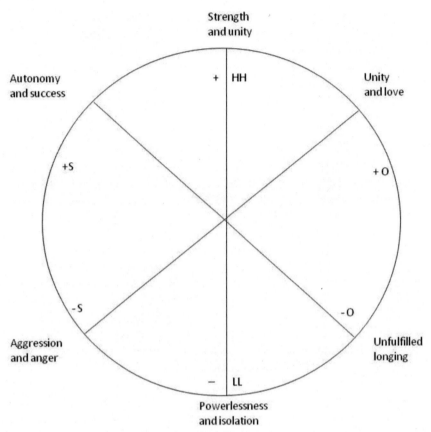

Figure 3.1. Circle of *I*-positions as rooted in basic motives.

- I as strong and inspired (+HH), associated with a high level of affect referring to self-assertion, high level of affect referring to contact and union and, at the same time, with many positive feelings. This affect combination emerges when one feels part of an accepting family, group or community, feels strong in direct connection to others, or is dedicated to some common goal or purpose. This kind of position is typical of enthusiastic and productive cooperation.

TWO BASIC MOVEMENTS IN THE SELF

A basic idea in Dialogical Self Theory is that the person is positioned in space and time. As involved in a process of positioning and counter-positioning, the self is moving in space. As engaged in a process of positioning and re-

EXERCISE 3.1

In this exercise you apply the circle of Figure 3.1 on yourself. You are invited to select one position which is most prominent in your life and another one which you feel as least prominent or neglected.

Question 1

When you look at the circle, which of the 6 positions do you see as most prominent in your present life? Can you describe in a few sentences the nature of this position, for example, by telling about a typical circumstance or event?

_____

_____

_____

Question 2

Can you refer in the circle to a position which is least prominent or neglected in your present life? Can you describe in a few sentences the nature of this position?

_____

_____

_____

Question 3

When you look at your two positions (most and least prominent), what in your life made the one more prominent than the other? Can you describe this in a few sentences?

_____

_____

_____

Question 4

Would you like to keep it the way it is or do you want to change the existing prominence? If you want to change it, which initiatives could you take? Can you describe them in a few sentences?

_____

_____

_____

Question 5

Are there any other positions in the circle which can be helpful to diminish the prominence of the first position or to strengthen the second position? Can you describe an initiative you would like to take in order to change the prominence of this position in your life?

_____

_____

_____

positioning, the self is moving through time. We can use the circle to depict some of these movements.

The circle allows one to explicate two basic movements in the self: from self-enhancement to contact and back and from positive to negative and back. As a co-therapist, I noticed that each of these movements could be blocked in a particular phase in one's life. Let's have a closer look at the main movements of the self with special attention to possible blockages.

A flexible movement *from self-enhancement to contact* (from the left to the right of the circle) is difficult for people who are strongly involved in making a career or who are biased to autonomy, achievement, rationality and control in their lives. When, in Bakan's terms, unmitigated agency is ruling one's position repertoire, it is likely that a flexible movement from self-enhancement to connection and contact is limited or even impossible.

Moving *from contact to self-enhancement* (from the right to the left of the circle) is problematic for people who have, for a great deal of their lives, sacrificed themselves in the service of others and never had the chance to build up something for themselves. We have found this impediment also in people who are overly dependent on others or have never learned to make decisions as an autonomous person.

The inability of moving *from negative to positive* (from the lower to the upper part of the circle) is a familiar finding in all those cases in which people find themselves imprisoned in negative (unpleasant) experiences. When they no longer feel able to enjoy the activities of everyday life that gave them pleasure in an earlier, happier period, they often formulate experiences which are associated with a high level of negative feelings and a low level of positive feelings. As far as they introduce positive experiences, they refer to some past events or situations in their lives from which they feel isolated in their present existence. As research has demonstrated (Van Geel, 2000), clients in psychotherapy report not only many experiences with a high level of negative affect, but they also with a low amount of positive self-enhancement affect, indicating that they lack, at least for some time, the resiliency and strength to cope with their problems in an autonomous way.

Over the years my colleagues and I were impressed by the fact that some people seemed to stick to their positive experiences, not allowing negative emotions as part of their selves and being aversive to sharing such emotions with others. Apparently, the movement *from positive to negative* (from the upper to the lower part of the circle) is somewhere inhibited by their need to limit their lives to positive experiences only, thereby avoiding any self-reflection or dialogue about the nature of negative feelings. In fact, we have not found many of them in our psychotherapeutic practice for the simple reason that they do not ask for assistance, being resistant to allowing and discussing negative experiences and shadow positions as part of their selves. As far as we know them from self-investigations in research settings, we found this "addiction" to positive feelings particularly in people who seem to be attached to comfort, and instant happiness, and who tend to avoid any exploration of negative experiences. Often, they used the notion of "positive thinking" in order to transform, as soon as possible, any negative experience into a positive one. As a result of their persistent attempts to keep themselves *out* of these experiences, they do not take the opportunity to go, as part of a self-exploration or self-reflection, *into* their negative experiences. In this way, they prevent themselves from finding out what the meanings of these experiences are, and from listening to the message of these experiences as a valuable source of information (Hermans & Hermans-Konopka, 2010).

The main thing that I learned from studying the movements on the circle and, more generally, from processes of therapeutic change is that *flexibility* is the key issue. It is the capacity to go into particular kind of position, to leave it, and to move to another position, in such a way that the requirements of the situation in which a position is triggered are taken into account. So, it is not so important to "have" a particular number of positions in your repertoire or to have more positions of one kind than of another one. It is more adaptive to move from self-assertion to contact and vice versa and from positive to negative and vice versa on the basis of a broad and flexible repertoire.

THE DIALOGICAL NATURE OF BASIC MOTIVES

In my work with the Self-Confrontation Method over the years, I was often writing about basic motives and applying them in practical situations. I felt encouraged to do so because clients found them very clarifying and recognized them as important orientations in their own lives. They saw the motives as relevant perspectives from which they could better understand many of their actions. Confronted with their manifold experiences, spread in time and space, they used the motives as a tool to bring order and direction in their lives, which would be otherwise distributed over a great variety of situations and positions.

However, from the moment that I started to develop the Dialogical Self Theory, I began to realize that the way the basic motives were described in the Self-Confrontation Method and in its underlying "Valuation Theory" was not sufficiently dialogical. The motives were understood as located in the self of the individual and influencing the content and organization of his or her experiences. There was, however, not much attention to the way in which two or more people, involved in communication, *respond to the motives of each other*. In order to make a step into the direction of a dialogical view on motivation, I give some examples which show how people respond to each other as motivated beings.

Two professionals, one male the other female, recently met each other and decided to cooperate in developing a training program. She is more experienced and older, while he is ambitious and younger. When he needs advice, he contacts her for advice and she is always motivated to give it, quickly and adequately. However, when he develops his skills and tells her enthusiastically about his progress, she becomes more reserved and is slower in responding to his e-mails. There is a striking difference between her enthusiasm to help him when he needs it, and her distance and lack of involvement when he becomes more successful. This change can be understood when we realize that initially she was placed in the position of helper, which gratifies both her self-enhancement motive ("I'm good in my profession") and contact-motive ("When he needs me, I'm there as I feel connected with him"). Later, however, when he becomes more successful, she arrives in the position of competitor ("I'm quite good, but he may become my equal or even better"). Their cooperation is at risk as they change from a fit to a misfit between their positions. This can be easily understood when we see that they make different movements on the circle. Initially, they cooperate on the basis of positions located at the top of the circle. In their enthusiasm they both experience strength and contact in their common enterprise. After some time, however, she is moving from the top of the circle to the left where she is experiencing an increasing amount of negatively felt competition or even envy (-S). From his side, he continues to stay on the top of the circle and continues to feel connected with her, at the same time being surprised that she becomes so distant when he wants to share his success and progress with her. The beginning of the misfit is in the moment that he, while becoming more successful, continues to expect to be supported by her, while she is no longer able to relate to him from her contact motive because she feels that he is becoming her rival.

The second example is just an observation. Some thirty years ago, I was an enthusiastic photographer, eager to take pictures whenever I was impressed by something. Once, during a vacation in France, I decided to visit the magnificent cathedral of Chartres. Approaching the entrance, I saw an old beggar sitting near the door of the church with crossed legs, asking for alms with slow and tiring movements. Looking at him, I was impressed by the stark contrast between the miserable state of the beggar and the wealth of the tourists who passed by indifferently. So, I decided to take a photo in the expectation that he, in this crowded place with many passing visitors, would not notice me. However, just before the click, he suddenly straightened his back, conjured up a broad smile on this face and, to my embarrassment, started to enthusiastically wave at me as if I was an old acquaintance. It was as if he became, in a split second, 20 years younger and seemed to be in good shape. Entirely confused, I gave up taking the picture and disappeared into the entrance of the cathedral. What happened in these few seconds? The man, as an experienced beggar, knew that he would collect the most money when he would place himself in the position of a miserable old man (the lowest position of the circle). However, he did not want me to take a photo of him in this position. So, he altered his appearance in such a way that he prevented me to do something which I wanted but which he did not want. In this way he was, at least for that short moment, in a winner position (+S), reducing me, at the same time, to a loser position (-LL). After all, he lectured me on how to play with positions.

Cultural factors are also important for the process of positioning and repositioning. I remember the story of a woman who was raised in a conservative environment somewhere in the south of Italy. After her university studies, she did a dissertation and decided to give presentations at international conferences, learning to express herself in the English language. In her story, she emphasized how learning English was important for her de-

---

EXERCISE 3.2

In this exercise you explore if there is a particular person or a group of people in your life with whom you can share or would like to share prominent or non-prominent positions as reflected by the circle?

Question 1
Is there somebody in your life with whom you would like to share your most prominent position? Can you tell in a few sentences what makes that you choose this person?

_____

_____

_____

Question 2
Is there somebody in your life with whom you would like to share your least prominent or neglected position? Can you tell in a few sentences what makes that you choose this person?

_____

_____

_____

velopment. Using that language helped her to feel more like an autonomous person than she ever felt when speaking in her mother tongue. Her husband, however, educated as he was on the basis of traditional role definitions, found it increasingly difficult to live with a wife who became increasingly autonomous. This led finally to their divorce. In making a career, she was involved in an internal fight against her traditional role as a woman, but, when she actually moved into that direction, her husband was no longer able to cope with her more autonomous position. While they married on the basis of traditional role model, she moved into the direction of a more modern role model. This created a misfit in their relationship. Changes of this type are, in many variations, typical of the process of globalization and its localization counter-part that create fields of tension for many social relationships. The traditional role definitions, in many cultures, do not give much space for the self-enhancement and self-development of women. Whereas the woman of our example participated increasingly in global networks, her husband remained attached to the role definition that was typical of his local, cultural situation. This created a field of uncertainty for both, in which they, as a married couple, could not find their way. In our era, we witness an increasing number of women all over the world, claiming a more autonomous position, a process that characterizes the change from traditional to modern and post-modern models of the self.[5]

Having these examples in the background, what does a dialogical relationship between motivated positions looks like? To put it briefly, the best condition in which dialogical relationships may emerge is one in which people, both as individuals and as representatives of their groups and cultures, give each other the *space* in which both their contact motive *and* their self-enhancement motive receive a developmental impetus. In this space they both feel encouraged to position themselves as connected and as free, as being part of a common history and as emerging from an individual history, and in which they feel free to give expression both to their positive and negative experiences in flexible ways.

The dialogical view, presented in this book, proposes that people learn to give space to self-enhancement and contact not only in the relationships *between* people, but also *within* the self of the individual person. That is, the person learns to develop in him- or herself both positions emerging from self-assertion (e.g. "I as free," "I as ambitious," or "I as competitive") and positions that find their motivational source in the contact motive ("I as feeling connected with my family," or "We as taking care of the future of our children"). The combination of "between" and "within" is based on the belief that in a globalizing world, dialogue can only unfold if it takes place not only between individuals and groups but also in the self as a "society of mind."

MY OWN POSITIONS REVISITED

A dialogical view of emotions may be useful to shed some light on my dreams reported in the beginning of the present chapter and also on the development of my ambitious position as reported in Chapter 2. As I discussed there, this position emerged initially as a compensation for my early feeling of being an inferior pupil and social outcast. After starting as a compensation, the ambitious position developed in a more autonomous way, becoming more independent from its origin. It became a promoter position that stimulated my intellectual and social development in later years.

From a motivational point of view, it should be noted that my ambitious position led me to compare myself with others in a way that showed that the needs of this position were virtually insatiable. I noticed that I, like many others, compared myself not so much with people who were less lucky, successful, or recognized, but typically with people who were "better." There are always people who are better and it is, for the ambitious position, particularly frustrating when the competitors are younger, brighter, and have achieved more recognition in professional circles or society than I have. I sometimes tried to "correct" my ambitious side, by arguing that Albert Bandura probably had much admiration for William James, who, in turn felt that he worked in the shadow of Plato, who in turn had the highest respect for Socrates, who finally had to poison himself. However, this "reasoning" was not very able to soften the pretentions of the ambitious position. I discovered that these "better people" received an established position as "others-in-the-self," stimulating my imagination about their grandiosity and putting myself down as not meeting the standards that I applied to my competitors. In this way, the imagined others, as external positions in my self, continually fed my internal ambitious position. That is, my ambition position did not simply produce a need that is fulfilled or not fulfilled, as one would expect on the basis of traditional motivation theories. Rather, "internalized" competitors, particular the superior ones, often appeared in my imagination and stimulated me to improve my plans, actions and performances. Moreover, these external positions as part of my own self constantly fed my ambitious position that, in fact, was never satisfied for long. The real dialogical element came when I was in contact with a few people, whom I loved and who loved me. They gave me the space to talk about my ambitious position so that I could externalize it and keep it at a certain distance so that it lost its permanent dominance in my life. Love was capable of accepting my ambitions and softening them, in this way making movements to the right of the circle as depicted in the present chapter.

Moreover, I could get along better with my ambitious position when I discovered that it could become part of new "coalitions." Rather than being suppressed or removed from the repertoire, the ambitious position can serve as a non-dominant partner in cooperation with "I as cooperative" or "I as creative." In this way, the ambitious one received the space to invest its energy in direct collaboration with other positions, which became increasingly influential within me in the course of time.

I started this chapter by depicting the dream of my "lost garden" that impressed me both by its meaningful character and frequency over the years. I never felt fully able to understand it. The present chapter can be seen as an attempt to give an interpretation. As I argued, it brought me to the conclusion that it is an archetypical experience of a particular kind: the lost paradise reflecting the existential imperfection or lack of being. From a motivational point of view, the last part of the dream is particularly significant to me. Central was the emotion of "total emptiness": this emptiness was reflected not only by the cold walls, the lack of green in the environment, and the rationality of the straight lines, but also by the lack of *life*: there was no blade of grass, no animal, and, first of all, there were no people in my environment. I was doomed to live in this spiritless environment for the rest of my life. I felt both powerless and isolated, as reflected by the lowest position on the circle (-LL). The experience associated with this position was not simply a non-fulfillment of the two motives, self-enhancement and contact, but its specificity could be better understood as an interactional process. The environment was "speaking" to me by its lack of something or somebody who should be there but was not, and this shortcoming further reinforced the desperate character of my need for contact. In this dream my inner space was entirely emptied and felt like a bare desert. I was searching for something in the environment but the environment "answered" with an all-pervasive "no" or "nothing." This "no" was a failing start of contact and prevented, as long as I was in that situation, any dialogue from emerging.

From my reflections on my dreams in this chapter and on the transformation from inferiority to ambition in the previous chapter, I learned that there are basic motives in the self which can be temporarily but never permanently fulfilled. We need a myriad of positions and counter-positions on our way to satisfy basic motives which, according to their intrinsic nature, can never be entirely gratified.

Metaphorically speaking, we are the half of a circle, longing to become a full one, while never fully and permanently reaching it. Sometimes we receive a glimpse of beauty or perfection in a dream or we feel fulfillment or delight for a certain period in our everyday life. Such sparkles or transient periods can give us moments of an extraordinary, and often unspeakable, beauty. The encounter with the other, in dream or reality, is an essential part of this experience. I consider this encounter as a form of non-verbal dialogue, in which question and answer, and giving and receiving coincide in one moment of blissful, mutual contact.

NOTES

1. This study is reported by Hermans, Hermans-Jansen, and Van Gilst (1985) who used a list of 30 affect terms to explore clients" stories about themselves in terms of a system of "valuations" (personal meaning units resulting from self-reflection). This list, including affect referring to self-assertion (S), connection with others (O), positive experiences (P) and negative experiences (N), was further examined by Van Geel and De Mey (2003), who used a principal component analysis in order to study its factorial structure.

2. The research on the Fugit Amor experience is detailed by Hermans and Van Gilst (1987).

3. For an overview of distinctions similar to autonomy vs. homonomy as applied to individuals and cultures in contemporary literature, see Hermans and Kempen (1998). For a recent criticism of the modern emphasis on the pursuit of self-esteem and control, see Crocker and Park (2004).

4. For psychometric evidence of the 6 types of valuations on the basis of principal component analysis, see Van Geel and De Mey (2003).

5. For extensive discussion of traditional, modern, post-modern, and dialogical models of the self, see Hermans and Hermans-Konopka (2010, chapter 2).

Chapter Four

Revolutions in the Self and the Phenomenon of Dominance Reversal

Continuity gives us roots; change gives us branches, letting us stretch and grow and reach new heights.

Pauline R. Kezer

I walked quietly along the posters exhibited in one of the rooms of the conference site. I looked with interest at the presenters who were discussing their research with their colleagues. Suddenly, the door opened and a woman entered. She immediately caught my attention. My first emotion was just surprise. She walked along the posters and was standing still at some of them. In the crowded room, I lost view of her, but sometimes I could see her walking around among the participants. It struck me that she addressed no one and was fully concentrated on the texts of the posters. Gradually, my initial surprise changed into intense interest. After some time, I, usually shy, did something unusual: I approached her and asked: "Do you find it interesting?" We became for some minutes involved in a conversation that gave me the feeling of being involved in a natural stream: it was flowing and it went spontaneously and without any artificial formality. I talked with her as with a person whom I knew for many years. In the middle of this conversation, a close colleague approached me, who was the organizer of a symposium that was starting after a minute. I decided to end the conversation with her and walked with my colleague to the symposium room. Walking with him side-by-side, I said half-loudly, as speaking more to myself than to him: "God, what is happening to me!?"

After the conference, one day was left before the end of my stay. I made an appointment with her to visit some of the cultural places in Warsaw together. We walked for 10 hours sharing many personal and professional experiences, which continued during our visits to galleries and restaurants. One of the most significant moments in our conversations was when we were walking along the "Barbakan," part of old Warsaw's fortifications and used as a town gate in the past. Talking about her experiences, she used the term "my inner space." At that moment I stood still because this expression aroused my strong interest. I never heard somebody talk about his or her "inner space," a concept that I recognized in my own self. Also from a scientific point of view, this concept was relevant to my thinking as I believe that space is not simply outside the self but that the "self" itself is a spatial construction, or better, a spatial process. After exchanging many memories and personal experiences, I brought her back to her place. We said farewell to each other but we exchanged our e-mail addresses.

The night following this long and unusually intense meeting, I had the feeling that I had gone deeply into the life and emotional world of another person and rediscovered there, reflected and enlightened by her, many of my own experiences. I could not sleep. It was as if I was in a feverish state, although I was not ill at all. I was trembling the whole night. I felt that something extraordinary was happening to me. It was as if I went far beyond the boundaries of my ordinary self, thrown into a kind of ego-less kind of existence. For the first time, in my life I was not afraid to die.

WHAT HAPPENED TO ME?

Since the impressive event with Agnieszka, I did not stop wondering what had happened to me. I found it too superficial to conclude that I simply was falling in love with her. It was certainly more. Something was not only happening between us, but, as I noticed later, also *within* us.

Reflecting on my meeting with Agnieszka, I found out that it evoked what I would like to call a "revolution" in myself. In order to understand this, I go back to a self-investigation with the use of the Personal Position Repertoire (PPR) Method (Hermans, 2001) that I had applied to myself several years before I met Agnieszka. One of the findings which struck me in particular was the basic structure in my position repertoire. It consisted of two groups of internal positions. One contained positions like "I as freedom seeker," "I as independent," "I as ambitious," "I as professional," and "I as scientist," "my masculine side" and, to my surprise, also the "avenger." The second group, clearly distinguished from the first one, included positions like "I as artistic," "I as a dreamer," "I as receptive," "I as in love," "I as spiritual," and "my feminine side." From a motivational point of view, the first group can be seen as an expression of the striving for self-assertion and self-enhancement

(S-motive), whereas the second group represents the longing for contact and union with somebody or something else (O-motive). The first group is clearly located at the left part of the circle of positions, as discussed in Chapter 3, while the second group corresponds to the right part.

Until my meeting with Agnieszka, the first group of positions was clearly prominent in my work and even in many of my personal contacts, while the second was rather neglected, although I had moments, typically when being alone, in which I felt in close contact with these positions. It was this second group that was directly, fully, and emotionally addressed in my meeting with Agnieszka. The special character of our meeting was that these positions were also present and appealed in her, giving us a sense of being "soul mates." The free expression and sharing of this second group of positions was so power-ful, that it felt as a "revolution" in both our selves.

In our conversations many months after our first meeting, Agnieszka and I came to a point where we discussed the subjective meaning of our names. She noticed that my name consisted of two parts: "Hu" and "bert," which represented different and even contrasting aspects of my self. While "bert" induced in her a red color, clearly visible at the foreground, active and ex-pansive, "Hu" evoked a blue color, more spatial, at the background, and of a more receptive nature. After walking around with her associations, I realized that, up till then, my social identity, the way I presented myself to the outside world, had always been like "Bert." Actually, Bert was my colloquial name which I adopted since I started my university studies when I was 22 years old. Although my official name was Hubert, which I used in publications only, everybody in my immediate environment called me "Bert." Agnieszka's as-sociations made me aware of the one-sided character of this name by which I presented my self-assertive, active side to the outside world only, with the neglect of the other side which had been always been so important to me, certainly as a young boy (see the dreamer in Chapter 2). In fact, had the feeling that I started my life as "Hu" but as the result of being bullied by my classmates at school and, moreover, under the influence of the intellectual climate of my school career, the dreaming and receptive positions had been increasingly suppressed by my social environment. The reflections on my name, and the symbolic meaning involved, helped me decide to present my-self as Hubert, which rooted me, at the same time, more in my family tradi-tion because it was the name of my grandfather.

The deeper background of the two parts of my name was expressed in an e-mail which I wrote to Agnieszka some time after our reflections about my name:

My impression is this: when you are socially isolated quite long, then you de-velop an inner world, an inner space as a livable alternative to the world which is not your best place. This is the place of your dreams and imaginations. This is the world into which you retreat. However, then you have to retreat from the social environment in which you are living as well. You find the best moments when you are reading a good book on your own and you enjoy making a walk on your own. Suddenly, there appears a person who breaks through the walls of your internal self. She is doing something which you never expected. After the break-through, this person accompanies you in going deeper into your inner world of dreaming and imagination and she joins you in going into that mysterious space, which becomes a common space and this is wonderful! This is the great surprise.

What happened to me is that meeting the person who went with me to the farther reaches of my inner self brought to the forefront something which was already present in the background of my self, but which could not be directly expressed in my relationships with other people. Most of my contacts with other people took place from the positions which originated from the self-enhancement motive. These positions and the interactions that emanated from them, gave me the self-esteem that I needed, after this esteem was put down by my early experiences of inferiority as described in Chapter 2. What happened to me is, on a basic level, the same as what happened to some of the participants in my research project on the dialogical self. This process can be summarized under the name of "dominance reversal."

DOMINANCE REVERSAL AND THE CHANGE OF MEANING

The phenomenon of dominance reversal reflects a radical change of the self, implying that *I*-positions that are present in the background of the repertoire become pushed to the foreground so that they become, temporarily or permanently, dominant in the self. Typically, external events (e.g., meeting a new person) or internal events (e.g., imaginations) *trigger* these radical changes rather than *cause* them. That is, dominance reversal as a process in the self that emerges *primarily* from the internal dynamics of the self, rather than being the result or effect of external factors. From the background of the repertoire, a particular position is putting the self under an increasing pressure, waiting to become expressed when the right external stimulus is there. The result is that it becomes dominant over the positions that were restraining the self up till that moment. A "small" external stimulus may have a strong effect, leading to a revolution in the self.

In my initial explorations of the dialogical self (Hermans & Kempen 1993), I posed to some college students the following question: "Do you see in your personality two opposite sides with one side as more dominant than the other?" My first research participant, Alice, a twenty-eight-year-old woman, told me that she saw the "open side" of her personality as most dominant and influential and she added that other people also saw her as an open person ("friendly," "helpful," and "sociable"). She further revealed that she also had another part, less acceptable to herself and less visible to others, that often was in conflict with her open part. She described this part as "my closed side." She emphasized that she had decided to become engaged in this investigation, because she was particularly interested in exploring her closed side as an unfamiliar aspect of herself.

In the next step of the investigation, Alice was invited to share some events and circumstances in her past, present, and expected future from the two *I*-positions successively. First, she told her story as an "open person" and then as a "closed person." From her open position she primarily told stories that referred to her warm and unproblematic relationship with her mother and to the positive aspects of the relationship with her boyfriend. From the perspective of her closed side, however, she largely referred to the problematic relationship with her father and expressed considerable doubts about the future with her boyfriend. Note that she described the relationship with her boyfriend from her open position in terms of "always," whereas from her closed position she had reservations that clearly deviated from any "always." When I compared the two groups of sentences, I learned that such a position exercise is very suitable to make conflicts, contradiction, and oppositions in the self explicit and to assist the person to become aware of the existence of inconsistencies and discontinuities in the self as a normal phenomenon.

ALICE'S STORIES FROM HER OPEN AND HER CLOSED POSITION[1]

Sentences from the Open Position

Past

1. My mother, open and cheerful, has always been like a friend to me.
2. In the past many friends visited our house: everything was allowed.

Present

3. The contact with my boyfriend: I'm always listening to him, I'm always there for him.
4. When there are problems in our family, I'm the one who is called, because I listen and am prepared to help.

Future

5. In the future I want to meet lots of people, get to know lots of people.
6. In the future I want to travel together with my partner; that makes me feel free.

Sentences from the Closed Position

Past

7. When I was 12 years old, my father left the house; I know so little about that period; I think there is much pain and sorrow during that time.
8. I have the feeling that I have never had a father.

Present

9. In the contact with my father I must show my limits; otherwise he completely overruns me; that makes me sad, but it is also a good learning experience.
10. My partner and I both had a broken relationship in the past: I do not want to lose myself again in another relationship.

Future

11. I would like very much to have children, but this is suppressed by other things (traveling, studying, work, freedom).
12. I need rest, no musts; would like to have just once an empty agenda.

After the investigation, I introduced a procedure that led to the discovery of a radical change in the self. I asked Alice to rate her stories about *dominance* ("How dominant was this aspect of your life during the past week?") and on *meaningfulness* ("How meaningful was this aspect of your life during the past week?"). She answered these questions for her thinking, feeling, and action separately. I was surprised to see that, over the three-week period, the sentences of her closed position became more dominant than the sentences of her open position, whereas the sentences of the latter position receded to the background (see Figure 4.1). This change represents a clear example of a "dominance reversal," also found in another study (Hermans 1996). Moreover, the findings showed that, in the same period, the meaningfulness of the sentences from Alice's closed position strongly increased, whereas the meaningfulness of the sentences from her open position considerably decreased (see Figure 4.2). Apparently, the increasing dominance of her closed position was experienced as very meaningful, although this position was

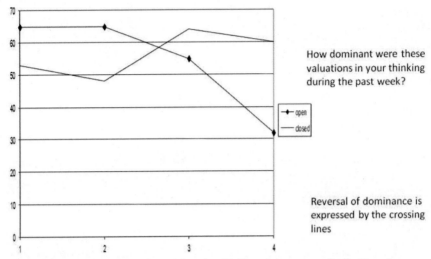

Figure 4.1. Average dominance ratings for thinking about personal valuations for *open* and *closed* positions over four weeks. From Hermans, H.J.M., & Kempen, H.J.G. (1993). *The Dialogical Self: Meaning as Movement.* San Diego: Academic Press. © Elsevier.

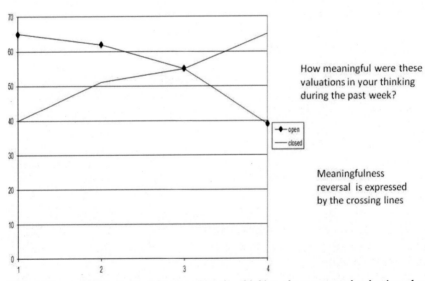

Figure 4.2. Average meaningfulness ratings for thinking about personal valuations for *open* and *closed* positions over four weeks. From Hermans, H.J.M., & Kempen, H.J.G. (1993). *The Dialogical Self: Meaning as Movement.* San Diego: Academic Press. © Elsevier.

associated with a great deal of negative emotions! I experienced this finding as particularly interesting from the perspective of psychological health. Why would a person become involved in the negative emotions (e.g., sadness and guilt) of a particular position ("closed") while she already had a very positive and meaningful one ("open") available? If her goal would be to have positive feelings only, then her open position would enable her to have them. Yet, she decided to go through a process in which this position became decreasingly meaningful while her closed, but negative, position was felt as increasingly meaningful. Why?

When she made her diary notes accessible to me after the period of investigation and we discussed them in combination with the findings as reported above, I could find some answers to these questions. Alice succinctly expressed it in this way:

> I think that I sometimes flee to that [open] side…Then I'm floating away from myself…*I become aware that an important part of myself is in that closed side*…I'm also beginning to see that when I express my vulnerable parts, I get much closer to other people, and then, it goes better with me too (Hermans & Kempen, 1993, p. 86, emphasis added).

As this quotation shows, Alice indicates that she feels the closed position as an important part of herself. Apparently, she wants to be a *whole person*, even when this requires her to go *into* her feelings of sadness and guilt associated with her closed position. I understood her remarks as bringing hitherto neglected or suppressed experiences to the surface, giving her a sense of unity or synthesis in her life as a whole. At the same time, this helped her to improve the relationships with other people, including her father and other family members. (She told that her participation in the investigation and the reflections it aroused, made her decide to get in touch with her father and brother with whom she had no contact for several years.)

Alice's self-investigation of her opposite sides is an example of the paradoxical nature of the multiplicity of the dialogical self, as noticed by Rowan (2010): the more we are going into our different parts, the more the self experiences itself as a whole.

JAMES'S NOTION OF UNSTABLE EQUILIBRIUM

I posed the question about the two opposite sides to approximately 25 students and I followed their changes over a period of three weeks. However, I found the phenomenon of dominance reversal, in different variations, only in a minority of them. I became curious to know why some of the cases showed the crossing lines and others not? After searching through some literature, I found an answer in one of the works of William James.

When James (1902/2004) was in the phase of studying conversions in the self of religious and non-religious people, he introduced a notion, "unstable equilibrium," that is particularly relevant to understanding the dynamic aspects of the self. In some periods of life, he found out, the self *seems* to be in a state of stability, but at a lower level of consciousness, there are one or more tendencies that are striving for expression. However, these tendencies are incompatible with the more dominant parts of the self which then leads to a state of instability. As the needs of the lower level are not met, the 'lower' parts put the self, over the course of time, under considerable pressure. Finally this results in a "conversion," whereby the hitherto dominant parts become overruled by the "revolting" parts.

In order to understand the phenomenon of unstable equilibrium better, let's have a look at a phenomenon that James describes under the term "falling out of love." He refers to a man who adored a girl with whom he had violently fallen in love. As many people in this state, the man fell into a regular fever and could not think of anything else. When he was alone, he constantly re-called his past conversations with her and was totally absorbed in his fanta-sies about heavenly meetings anticipated in the future. However, pretty and attractive as she was, she was surrounded by a group of admirers to whom she used to respond from a "spirit of coquetry." Somewhere *in the back of his mind*, the man knew that she was unfit to be a good wife for him and even expected that she would not say "yes" when he would ask her for a marriage. At some moment, James describes, there was a sudden change:

> The queer thing was the sudden and unexpected way in which it all stopped. I was going to my work after breakfast one morning, thinking as usual of her and of my misery, when, just as if some outside power laid hold of me, I found myself turning round and almost running to my room, where I immediately got out all the relicts of her which I possessed, including some hair, all her notes and letters, and ambrotypes on glass. The former I made a fire of, the latter I actually crushed beneath my heel, in a sort of fierce joy of revenge and punish-ment. I now loathed and despised her altogether, and as for myself I felt as if a load of disease had suddenly been removed from me. That was the end (James, 1902, p. 180).

James compares such reversal processes with the proverbial last straw added to the camel's burden. There was an internal process of accumulation that finally reached a point of oversaturation, like the touch of a needle which makes the salt in a supersaturated fluid suddenly crystallize. In such a state of unstable equilibrium a "small" event, such as an innocently seeming remark from another or even an internal thought, leads to the revolution of central parts of the self or of the self as a whole. The state of unstable equilibrium is solved, at least for some time, and is transformed into a state of balance.

Apparently, the state of unstable equilibrium is a fertile soil for a dominance reversal in the self. A particular position or group of positions are dominant in the self for some time, while at a lower level of consciousness there are one or more other positions that are conflicting with the dominant one. The "lower" positions are not yet strong enough to become dominant. However, as long as the lower positions are neglected or suppressed by the higher ones and their needs not met, there is a growing dissatisfaction and stress in the self as a whole. The lower positions can only come to the surface and even become dominant when they strengthen their pressure (as a result of increasing frustration) or when they establish a coalition with other positions so that as a group they are stronger than as agencies in isolation.

James's example of falling out of love and my experience of falling in love, seem to be opposite on a manifest narrative level. However, on a deeper positional level they are expressions of the same process. In both cases, positions (e.g., "I as abused" in James's example and "I as a dreamer" in my case) that were for some time piling up energy in the background of the self, finally led to a dominance reversal in the existing organization of the self to reach a new state of equilibrium.

The Struggle between the Dieter and the Cake Eater

In a discussion of the multiplicity of sub-selves, social-psychologist Bloom (2008) points out that the question "Are you happy?" is a problematic one as long as different parts of the self have different needs and interests. When such differences are evident (and they are) the happiness of one part of the self may run counter to the happiness of the other part. The happiness of the one leads to the misery of another part. A person who invests a lot of effort in his achievements, comes to a point that he wants to have some leisure, but when he goes for holiday, he may feel uneasy or even guilty because he has the feeling that he performs nothing. Or, a mother who spends a lot of her time raising her children, may want to build up something for herself. However, when she decides to participate in an educational training program, she feels guilty that she is not at home.

Drawing on studies about dieting, Bloom (2008) plots the relative strength of two competing parts of the self, the "dieter" and the "cake eater" in order to make sense of their interaction. He starts with a situation in which the dieter is stronger than the cake eater. For most of the day, the dieter is in regular power, indicated by a 5 on a scale of 1 to 10. Motivated by the long-term goal of weight loss, the dieter is dominant over the cake eater, the latter one having an intensity level of 2. As long as the dieter in myself is stronger than the cake eater, I'm firm in my decision not to eat the cake. However, as I get closer and closer to the cake and its seducing smell reaches my nostrils, the power of the cake eater rises (3…4…). At some point the lines cross and the cake eater takes over the power (level 6). From that moment on, the cake eater becomes my dominant *I*-position. At this point, I decide to eat the cake. At this moment of "dominance reversal" I'm not simply overwhelmed by an impersonal need that is stronger than "me." No, I decide to eat the cake. It is me who wants that. I'm not simply seduced by the delicious cake or determined by its smell. Rather, at some point I *let* myself be seduced. In doing so the cake eater is cleverer than we

---

EXERCISE 4.1
Do you remember a moment or period in your life in which you were subjected to a dominance reversal in yourself? Think of such examples as: feeling the urge to leave something important in your life behind you, or being involved for a long time in a social relationship and feeling an increasing urge to step out. Focus on your own experience, which may be very different from the given examples.

Question 1
Can you describe this change in some detail: What happened? Where? When?
_____
_____
_____

Question 2
Describe the positions of yours that were involved:Which position was dominant initially and which position became dominant after the break-through? Give a name to each of the two positions.
_____
_____
_____

Question 3
To what extent did you find this change meaningful and, if so, what made it meaningful?
_____
_____
_____

might think. He invents, on the spur of the moment, credible reasons for taking the decision to eat: "Ah, tomorrow is a better moment to start again" or "The exception confirms the rule," or "My grandmother became 92 and never cared about such things." The *I* is not above or outside the "lower" needs of the self or, at some later moment, overpowered by them. No, the *I* itself takes the decision and knows quite well how to find reasons for its justification. As Bloom notes, the flesh is not weak but clever.

When the dieter, with its long-term concerns, hands over its power to the cake eater, it retreats for some time to the background of the position repertoire, feeling ashamed or guilty about its failure to realize its purposes. What can the dieter do to keep the strings of power in his own hands? Expecting that it will later be dominated by another position when being in a similar situation, it can act to block the crossing by an act known as "self-binding" (Elster, 1989). Self-binding means that the dominant position protects itself against another position that might take control at some later point in time. Bloom refers to the classic example of Ulysses who desired to hear the seductive song of the sirens, but he knew it would compel him to walk into the sea. Therefore, he commanded his sailors to tie him to the mast. Dieters practice self-binding by deciding to buy food in small portions so they won't overeat later on. Alcoholics avoid bringing alcoholic beverages into their households and smokers try to quit by telling their friends never to give them a cigarette. When making a hotel reservation, some people demand to have a room with an empty mini-bar. Today, there are alarm clocks for sale that roll away as it sounds the alarm. To shut it off, one has to go out of bed and search for the mobile clock somewhere in the room. What these examples have in common is that one position that is dominant in the self takes measures to prevent other positions from assuming power at some later moment.

DOMINANCE REVERSAL IN THE LIFE COURSE:
THE CASE OF A "DISSIDENT" BISHOP

While the case of the dieter usually takes place within a limited time frame, the phenomenon dominance reversal can reflect sudden and unexpected changes in the course of life. It happens, for example, when people who were for a long time successful in a particular job, suddenly decide to turn and go into a different direction.

During the nineties of the last century, the most well-known bishop in The Netherlands, Martinus Muskens, was the leader of one of the southern dioceses in the country. He caused a national sensation, particularly in the circles of bakers, with his remark that a poor person who is hungry is well permitted to steal bread. Emotions were running high when he, in the presence of a television crew, slept one night on a street in Amsterdam as an act of solidarity with the vagabonds of the city. With this performance he tried to direct attention to the fact that, in a time of prosperity, there is a relatively large number of people who live in poverty. He confirmed his fame as a "dissident bishop" by presenting himself as an advocate of the use of condoms in the service of AIDS prevention and by proposing to disconnect celibacy from the priesthood. Some people considered his actions and statements as deviating from the rules and traditions of the Catholic church, while others rewarded him with warm support, considering his proposals as signs of a deeply felt Christian inspiration.

To the surprise of many, he resigned from his position as bishop in 2007 and decided to enter a monastery in the order of the Benedictines with the intention to spend the rest of his life as a humble monk. Why did he make such a sudden move? From his time in the seminary, the young man had always "two souls in his breast": a pastor and a monk, the first one pushing him into the world, the second pulling him out of the world. As a pastor he travelled many years through Europe and Asia, as an active and dedicated missionary. After his appointment as bishop in 1994 he devoted his full energy to his pastoral work. However, two light strokes in 1999 and a slow revalidation forced him to work at a lower level of energy, although still able to do his duties. Finally, after writing a book on the theme of death, he decided, several years before the end of his official period, to retreat from his function as bishop and to enter the monastery (Broers, 2007).

I see the decision of bishop Muskens in making the transition from pastor to monk as an example of dominance reversal during the life course. During most of his career the pastor was dominant but the monk position always stayed at the background of his repertoire, waiting for the right moment to come to the fore. The light strokes were not a cause for the reversal but rather a trigger. It facilitated his decision to devote the rest of his life to something he had always wanted to so, but actually did not realize because the dominant pastor position prevented him from doing so. By bringing forward a significant part of himself that was neglected for a long time, he started, in the last part of his life, a new exploration.

A similar reversal of dominance can be observed in many people who retire from their job. Even when they have the opportunity to continue the same work, with less formal obligations, they decide to devote their energy to a very different activity. The retirement does not necessarily force them to give up their work, which used to give them so much satisfaction and pleasure. Rather, the retirement is an occasion for the break-through of hidden positions that were long waiting to become realized. As the example of the bishop demonstrates, some people take such a decision even before their official period or duties come to an end.

EXERCISE 4.2

Now let's go to your present life. There are two possibilities. You are presently in a state of unstable equilibrium or in a state of stable equilibrium. With the following questions we explore which of the two possibilities applies.

Question 1

Do you have a vague feeling that there is, in the background of yourself, a need that is important to you and which is there for some time, but is not or not yet fulfilled? Is it possible for you to describe this need in the form of an *I*-position ("I as needing…" or "I as desiring…")?

_____

_____

_____

Question 2

Is there another position in yourself that prevents the background position from coming to the foreground and becoming fully expressed? Can you describe this position ("I as…")?

_____

_____

_____

Question 3

To what extent do you feel a tension in yourself, given the fact that the background position is not fully expressed or developed? Can you describe the nature of this tension and how you respond to that?

_____

_____

_____

Question 4

When you have the feeling that you are in a state of *stable* equilibrium, can you describe the feelings associated with this state? Are you happy and relaxed with it or do you feel the need to change it?

_____

_____

_____

Revolutions in Self and Society

In developing Dialogical Self Theory, I was always interested in the comparison between self and society, on the assumption that the self can be fruitfully studied and even developed as a "society of mind." This interest led me to search for commonalities between the phenomenon of dominance reversal as a psychological phenomenon and the notion of revolution as a political process. The great variety of literature on political revolutions and the apparent differences in theoretical perspectives on the subject (e.g., Goldstone, 1993) make it a hazardous to draw firm conclusions. Yet, I want to sketch some similarities between dominance reversal and revolution, as an invitation for continued thinking and theorizing.

In the footsteps of Talcott Parsons and other sociologists, a variety of researchers see society as a system in *equilibrium* between various resources, demands and subsystems (political, cultural, etc.). Although these theorists often disagree on the causes of revolutions, they agree on the observation that it is a state of a severe *disequilibrium* that is responsible for revolutions, such as the French Revolution (1789–1799), the Russian Revolution of 1917 and the Chinese Revolution (1927–1949).

Another group of scientists, primarily in the political sciences (e.g., Charles Tilly and Samuel P. Huntington) consider revolutions as outcomes of a power struggle between competing interest groups. According to this view, revolution takes place when two or more groups cannot come to terms within the conventional decision making process of a political system, having at the same time sufficient resources available to use force in pursuing their goals. The relevance of this view for our purposes is that the notion of "power" is introduced, useful to describe social processes in which particular groups try to become dominant over others.

Particularly relevant to the phenomenon of dominance reversal is the observation that both the sociological and the political science groups, as summarized above, see revolutions as a two-step process. First, there is some change in society that results in a situation that is different from the past (e.g. economical, military, demographical, or technological changes). Second, the new situation provides an *opportunity* for a revolution to take place. In this situation that functions as a kind of "fertile ground" for a revolution to take place, an *event* that in the past would not have sufficient influence to cause a revolution (e.g., a bad harvest or a riot or a suicide), is now sufficient to do so. In other words, when the right time is there, the new situation provides the opportunity for an event to trigger, rather than to cause, a revolution. A recent example is the suicide of a fruit seller in Tunisia, an event that is generally seen as sparking the Arab spring in 2010.

THE SELF AS A DYNAMIC SOCIETY OF MIND
AND THE ROLE OF DOMINANCE AND POWER

When I look back at my first meeting with Agnieszka, I see my increasing need to express my receptive positions as an opportunity or new situation, in which my meeting with her had an impact that this event would probably not have had in some earlier period of my life. In Alice's case, her increasing need to know the dark side of herself led to a situation in which her self-investigation was enough to create a dominance reversal in herself. In James's story of the man falling out of love, the frequent flirting of his girlfriend created a new situation for him, in which his pessimistic thoughts about her stimulated him to suddenly turn home and destroy all her relics. In the case of the dieter, his increasing appetite made that the smell of the cake became so irresistible that he actually decided to eat. In all these cases there were changes that brought the self into a "dispositional state," in which a seemingly "innocent" event (a meeting, an investigation, a smell) had an unexpected strong effect that led to a reorganization of the self. In view of the similarities between the reorganization of the self and political revolutions, I propose to see the phenomenon of dominance reversal as a smaller or larger "revolution" in the self. Along these lines, I would propose for future research to look further at the basic commonalities between societal processes on the macro-level and psychological phenomena on the micro-level, in order to better understand the functioning of the self as a society of mind.

The society-metaphor has the apparent advantage that the self can be studied as a social and societal process in which social power plays a central role, as argued by Callero (2003). After listing and analyzing a series of psychological self-concepts in contemporary mainstream psychology (e.g., self-monitoring, self-efficacy, self-regulation, self-presentation, self-control), he concluded that the notion of social power is conspicuously missing. However, this notion is indispensible for understanding the workings of the self:

> "... the self that is socially constructed is never a bounded quality of the individual or simple expression of psychological characteristics; it is a fundamentally social phenomenon, where concepts, images, and understandings are deeply determined by relations of power. When these principles are ignored or rejected, the self is often conceptualized as a vessel for storing all the particulars of a person" (p. 127).

Social power and dominance are indispensible concepts not only in the analysis of revolutions in the classical-historical sense of the term, like the French and the Russian revolution. They are also essential to understanding the implications and consequences of the pervasive processes of globalization and localization in which our selves are continuously participating as exemplified by the increasing power of multi-nationals, the dramatic demographic changes as a result of contemporary immigration waves, the emergence of supra-national organizations (e.g. the European Union), the struggle of sub-national groups to attain political independence (e.g., Basque-nationalism or the Tamil Tigers in Sri-Lanka), and the clashes between religious groups (e.g., North-Ireland and Israel).

As we have tried to demonstrate in a previous publication (Hermans & Hermans-Konopka, 2010), the processes of globalization and localizations have significant implications for the organization of the self and for the position repertoire in particular. We argued that the increasing complexity of the (world) society has the consequence that also the individual self becomes more complex. As a result of globalization, the number and heterogeneity of the positions in the self tend to increase. We are getting more and more used to such examples as a young German studying in USA, a child raised by parents from different races, religions, or cultural backgrounds, an English scientist working for a company in India, a Catholic French woman married to a Jewish man raised in Israel, or a Polish family adopting a child from Haiti. My hypothesis is that *as a result of the increasing cultural, economic, ecological, political, demographic, ideological and military border-crossings in a globalizing society, the chance of dominance reversals in the self tends to increase.* In simple terms, when the person is developing some of his positions, there are always positions in one or another corner of the self waiting, or even pressing, to receive attention and to become realized. Because it is not possible to realize all positions at the same time, the needs and interests of the "waiting positions" increase stress in the self. When the situation of the self changes, a minor stimulus or event is then strong enough as a trigger for dominance reversal. When, as a result of globalization, the self is influenced by the values and practices of other local groups in the world and, consequently, different positions are striving for priority, the chance of "revolutions" in the self increases.

The increasing probability of dominance reversals in the self in contemporary society has a pervasive influence on the nature of social relationships. Suppose two or more people are working or living together. They both are subjected, from time to time, to unpredicted dominance reversals as they take place in a heterogeneous position repertoire. When this happens on both sides of an interaction, it leads to an increase of instability in the communication, particularly when participants have their origin in different cultures and different *I*-positions in the background of their position repertoire. In a post-modern, globalizing world, the probability of dominance reversals is considerably higher than in a traditional, homogeneous society, where people share a common (national) history, are raised in the same religious traditions and trained in the same cultural environment.

The increasing social instability resulting from unpredictable dominance reversals in the self requires, in my view, increasing dialogical skills. Given different social and cultural backgrounds, people are confronted, often at unexpected moments, with different sides of each other which they often don't know in advance. Dialogical skills are required in order to give space to the often unfamiliar experiences and emotions of each other, to understand them in their proper social and cultural context and to find ways to respond to them in adequate and flexible ways.

NOTE

1. From Hermans, H.J.M., & Kempen, H.J.G. (1993). *The Dialogical Self: Meaning as Movement.* San Diego: Academic Press. © Elsevier.

Chapter Five

Uncertainty

A Burden or a Gift?

Maturity of mind is the capacity to endure uncertainty.

John Finley

When I look back at my life, I always have the feeling that I lived in three different "worlds": the traditional world of a late-medieval village, the modern life of personal growth and achievement, and the post-modern participation in an international network. These worlds impressed me as strikingly different and, in their combination, laden with tensions. Let's have a look at the first one.

LIVING IN A TRADITIONAL WORLD

My mother was raised in a village nearby a city in the south of the Netherlands where my father was born. Very often I went with her and my brothers to the village to be together with my grandfather and grandmother. They lived a life that was not very different from medieval times. They had meat from their pigs, eggs from their chickens, milk from their cows, vegetables from their estates, horses to plough them, and fruits from their own meadows. Surrounded by curious grandchildren, my grandfather used to bake bread in a hard-stone oven which had a central place in the yard. As children we enjoyed this environment particularly because it provided us with an ideal playground where we could make big fires and "shot" each other with rotten apples and tough potatoes. Everything happened in close connection with a Walden-like, natural environment.

The lives of our grandparents were strikingly stable and organized in traditional ways. They behaved according to the strict rules of the church, obeyed the moral commands of the pastor, had a high appreciation of the school led by authoritarian teachers, and participated, together with all other villagers, in the yearly colorful folkloristic customs and festivals. They used to travel by a a horse-drawn cart not more than 8 kilometers in order to visit the nearby city, a special event for which they dressed themselves in official black clothes. In his most prosperous period, my grandfather was rich enough to buy a car. In a photo I see my grandfather, sitting with a white stand-up collar behind the steer of an early model of a Ford, with a very proud expression on his face with the awareness that he was the first person of his village who owned such a precious vehicle. However, even more than property, descent determined one's status in the village. During conversation when the participants talked about a particular person, they referred to that person according to patrilineal descent. So, my mother was designated as "Netteke" from "Fonske" from "Pietsche" from "Klaoske," that is, as the last one of four generations in her father's line. People's identity, status and esteem were highly dependent on their descent. It was not the richest person, or the one with the highest education, or the highest achiever who was at the top of the community, but the person of noble descent. When I reflect on that time in my life, it strikes me that I was a part of a *traditional* community with a (late) medieval style of life.

LIVING IN A MODERN WORLD

Another "world" opened itself when I went to school. At primary school, and even more so at high school, individual achievements were highly valued. I wanted my parents to be proud of me, their eldest son, and I myself wanted to be recognized by my teachers and peers, particularly after the period in which I failed at school (Chapter 2). My growing achievement motivation, which initially functioned as a compensation for my early fiasco at school, was further stimulated by the competitive nature of the educational system. I remember that the teachers at primary school rewarded good behavior, effort and high achievements by giving their pupils beautifully colored cards. The more cards you collected, the "better" you were and the more your self-esteem flourished. In addition, the comparison of pupils on the basis of their marks at school generated an atmosphere of competition. Later, during my university time, this pursuit of high performance and self-esteem led me write a dissertation on "achievement motivation." Elaborating on this work, I developed a test for measuring three motives: achievement motive, debilitating anxiety, and facilitating anxiety. From the publications of David McClelland I learned that the achievement motive can be described in terms of "competition with a standard of excellence" as manifested in three forms: doing better than yourself at some earlier point in time, doing better than your peers or colleagues, and making progress in order to achieve some objective goal (e.g. becoming a doctor). Finally, I reached that goal: I became a full university professor, not being aware that this was just another step or even a new beginning of a next period of striving for excellence. I was just participating in another frame of reference. I wanted to be a "good" and "clever" professor, in comparison with my colleagues. I discovered that the permanent pursuit of excellence is a source of pleasure as long as you are successful, but a Sysiphus labor when you become aware that every achievement is followed by the (endless) pursuit of new accomplishments. After all, I see this "new world" of progress and individual competence as an expression of a *modern* self, given its emphasis on personal autonomy, training in rationality, emphasis on individual achievements and competition.

LIVING IN A POST-MODERN WORLD

My third "world" opened itself when I started to write in English and, years later became the chair of the scientific committee of the international conferences on the dialogical self. Every two years I contacted some colleagues in another country to find out if they were willing to organize this event in their country. From that time on, I was only partly in control of the course of affairs. Often organizers had styles of work that were different from mine and from each other, so every two years I had to deal with another group of people with whom I had an intense but passing working relationship. Often I just had to wait for what happened and, to my surprise, most of the time it went quite well because my colleagues abroad often showed unexpected tenacity for dealing with problems and possibilities. Gradually, I found myself to be part of a network of colleagues with whom I cooperated without much face-to-face contact. The contacts were mainly via e-mail and internet, and only sometimes were there meetings where we met in person. I started to live in a virtual world and participated increasingly in networks across the borders of countries and cultures.

Writing publications in another language and preparing international conferences in different countries led to actions that were not so much individual achievements but rather collaborative performances emerging from transnational and transcultural networks. Participating in this world brought its typical rewards and frustrations. There were colleagues who gave significant and lasting contributions to the further development of Dialogical Self Theory. There were also those who cooperated on a come and go basis. Some of them seem to disappear before I had even met them face-to-face. Sometimes I had the feeling that I was a player in a theatre who interacted with colorfully dressed characters who then suddenly appeared from the backstage to become involved in stimulating interactions. At the next moment, some of them disappeared unexpectedly in order to never come back. I worked and lived in this expanded and partly virtual reality often with enthusiasm and feeling closely connected with people far away, but sometimes also feeling disappointed and isolated. My experience of this world can be characterized by a combination of these adjectives: fluent, transient, unexpected, uncertain, virtual, and crowded. My experiences reflected what is usually designated as the *"post-modern* self."[1]

LIVING IN THREE WORLDS AT THE SAME TIME AND THEIR FIELDS OF TENSION

When I talk about the three "worlds" in which I lived, it may erroneously suggest a purely successive participation. Certainly, I was part of the traditional world of my grandparents before I entered my period as a modern "self-made man," and the latter one preceded my becoming part of a post-modern network society. However, the traditional phase did not stop when the modern one started and the modern phase continued during the emergence of the post-modern one. In my life I witnessed the *simultaneity* of the three worlds and I experienced this simultaneity sometimes as striking differences and agreeable variations but at other times as contradictions and conflicts to which I could only give an adequate answer after a period of uncertainty. I want to restrict myself here to two examples, one on the interface of the traditional and the modern world and the other on the interface of the modern and post-modern world.

During the time of writing this book, I'm living in the neighborhood of Nijmegen, a university city to which I moved 50 years ago and where I worked until my retirement as university professor. During half a century, I used to visit my place of birth, Maastricht, on a regular basis. In the course of time, many family members died and the previous generation gradually disappeared. However, my three brothers and I continue keep the tradition alive. Our aunt Mary, "the last of the Mohicans" of the previous generation, is always present in our meetings. We share stories about the past, with our parents and grandparents as central protagonists. We used to talk, sometimes with photos in our hands, about all those colorful figures of the past, about sad or humorous events and often we retell them as if they need to be revitalized after some time. Telling and re-telling them, sharing them, and joking about them gives a new glance to happenings that would otherwise be buried under a thick layer of dust. It's like travelling backwards in time, to the foggy spaces of the past. When I stop my work for a day and disconnect myself from any network, the meetings with my family members bring me back not only to many exciting events, but also to another "life world." Our family contact, memory and imagination cooperate with each other to relive the past. The monthly meetings feel like an entrance to situations and traditions in which our ancestors were once involved. I experience these meetings and the shared stories as a continuation and revival of the family traditions of the past.

The second example refers to the simultaneity of elements of what I described as the modern and post-modern world in which I was and still am living. I see my work—development of theory, methods, and applications—as originating from my modern self. I always wanted to develop something in which I could express my *personal* interests and capacities. This work was an expression of an autonomous mind that wanted to develop itself as an intellectual and to have some impact on his scientific and professional environment. When I entered my third world in which I became a member of an international network, I started more cooperative projects than ever before. However, my autonomous self that wanted to excel and influence my social environment did not disappear and did not even become less pretentious. On the contrary, it found in the networks new possibilities for self-improvement and self-expansion that originally derived from my modern autonomous self. So, I developed a kind of hybrid combination of a modern and post-modern self, sometimes leaning over to the one side, at other times gravitating to the other side, and even behaving as an undifferentiated mixture of modern and post-modern elements. Apparently, my modern self did not stop when my post-modern self emerged. At the same time, my traditional position remained at the background in order to become activated according to a regular schedule. Together, the three positions formed a self with a certain degree of personal and social complexity.

The Uncertainty of Living at the Borders

I sketched the three worlds in which I'm living with the purpose of making a statement that functions as a starting point of the present chapter: Living simultaneously in three "worlds"—traditional, modern, and post-modern—creates fields of uncertainty, because they are associated with values, needs and life-styles that are not only different but even mutually contradicting. Let me give an example from my own experience referring to the interface of the traditional and the modern self, as described in a previous publication (Hermans & Hermans-Konopka, 2010):

> I received my primary school education in the 1940s and 1950s of the previous century from teachers who were living as religious brothers in a monastery located in the neighborhood of my parents' house. The education was strictly

Catholic. Every morning the brothers, clothed in their dark habits, started their lessons with prayers followed by religious instruction and biblical stories in which they emphasized the normative implications for the everyday life of the pupils. They told us about the heavenly rewards that were promised for "right behavior," but also about the hellish punishments that waited for us if we lived a life of sin and lack of self-discipline. In accordance with the teachings, I believed that the Catholic religion was the "only true one" and that all other religions and worldviews were erroneous. However, when I was 14 years old, a sudden insight emerged from my own thoughts. Sitting alone in silence at home, I became immersed in a thought that came somewhere from the deeper layers of my mind. It came to me as a sudden awareness and had the character of a "flash" as Kohnstamm (2007) would call it. The thought took this form: *"When the representatives of other religions are as convinced about the truth of their beliefs as we are, then we can never have the only true religion."* This thought was not something that I remembered as coming from somebody else. It felt as though it came from me as a separate being, from the inner realms of my own mind and as the product of my earlier thinking and exploration. The thought was as precious as it was inescapable and it has left indelible traces in my mind ever since. Certainly, I was aware of the contradiction between my personal thought and the religious doctrines and dogmas of the Church, supported as they were by my beloved parents. Yet the thought did not make me an "unbeliever" or an "atheist." Rather, the contradiction evoked a continuing internal dialogue over the years, transforming the traditional religious beliefs of my early youth into a more personal quest. I became what one could call an "agnostic with a religious suspicion." Neither my interest in logical and scientific thinking nor my quest for spirituality disappeared over time. Instead, I remained committed to both of them for the rest of my life, although I was never able to resolve, what I saw as, their mutual tensions and conflicts. Rather, these tensions and conflicts functioned as an incentive to continue exploring both the field of science and spirituality (Hermans & Hermans-Konopka, p. 97).

Apparently, the education I received from my teachers in primary and high school had two sides. As teachers of language, mathematics, history, and other subjects, they encouraged their pupils to develop their reason and rationality, faculties at the heart of the modern self. At the same time, they represented an orthodox religious worldview that, not very different from Dante's medieval depiction of heaven and hell, contained basic elements of a traditional view of self and world. As indicated by my autobiographical memory, I applied the capacities of reason and argument to traditional religious dogmas, which created a field of uncertainty. This field provided a fertile ground for a dialogical interchange between two *I* -positions, "I as a thinker" and "I as religious." The two positions pulled me into entirely different directions, the religious one was used to "believe" without any critical questioning, while the thinker wanted to argue and wanted to see proof on the table. The dialogue between them led at some point to a "dominance reversal." The religious position, established in my mind as the result of my education, had to give way to the thinking position that was of great value to my autonomous self. The thinking position challenged the religious one by a critical interrogation of its dogmas and beliefs. Although the thinker was dominant in the ongoing dialogue, the believer did not disappear but was rather transformed into a more open and (re)searching spiritual position.

Another experience, on the interface of the modern and post-modern, also illustrates the emergence of a field of uncertainty. Some years ago, a colleague contacted me, asking me to prepare a text to be published in Wikipedia. I wrote the text with the implicit expectation that I was the author, the only one. After publication, however, I discovered that other people, whom I did not know at all, entered the site and made changes in the existing text, which I as the original author had submitted and they did so without consulting me. Rationally, I knew that this procedure was in perfect agreement with the rules of Wikipedia which is set up as a "democratic dictionary." Yet, I was irritated because I experienced the often anonymous contributors, coming out of the blue and often presenting themselves with nicknames, as intruders to *my* text. Later I understood that this event was an example of what the French philosopher Roland Barthes would call the "death of the author." In his view, the meaning of a particular work is not so much produced by an individual author but by his audience. The author is no longer the "authority" of the text, but his readers, in their interpretation of the text here and now, recreate and even rewrite it. I understood this view on texts in an intellectual way, but I felt confused as it brought me into a field of uncertainty. As a representative of a modern self, with its celebration of autonomy and individuality, I believed that the authority of the author was an incontrovertible principle. On the other hand, as a representative of a post-modern self, I participated in a network that required me to give up the exclusive rights of my authorship and give my text away to a broader readership that, at any moment, had the power to recreate, reshape and change "my" original formulations, even without asking my opinion.

Finally, I found out that the field of uncertainty originating from my double position as autonomous author and network participant was more productive than I had expected. I had to admit that my original text, by the contributions of people whom I originally saw as intruders, was often improved and became more accessible to a broader audience.

The experience of living in three worlds, including their mutual tensions and conflicts, did not only create fields of uncertainty but also stimulated my later interest in the multiplicity of the self. Each of the three worlds had its own atmosphere and left different traces in my mind. The traditional world made and still makes me feel rooted and connected with the lives of my family and ancestors, the modern world invites and even forces me to struggle and to find my place in an achieving society, and the post-modern world makes me aware that my autonomy is only partly "my own ground." It is rather a ground that is open to all sides so that many kinds of people, from different origins and cultures can come in without ringing the bell.

TOLERANCE OF UNCERTAINTY

It often strikes me that many politicians, teachers and captains of industry, when they notice an increasing level of uncertainty in their organizations, say that the best remedy is to *give* people more certainty. This is, in my view, a miscalculation. Certainty is not something which can be provided like a food supplement or a cookbook instruction. Rather, it emerges when people receive the opportunity to give their personal, dialogical *answer* to uncertainty and cope with it in adaptive ways. This coping with uncertainty requires, first of all, a *tolerance* of uncertainty. This tolerance strikes me as one of the most needed and most necessary capacities for our time and for the future. Uncertainty is there, always and everywhere. Let's therefore have a look at this capacity in some more detail, first by considering it from the perspective of individual differences.

How Do People Differ in Tolerance of Uncertainty?

As psychologists we know that there are significant individual differences in tolerance of uncertainty. One of the most influential studies in this area was Adorno and colleagues' (1950) study on the *Authoritarian Personality*. Having escaped from Europe during the Nazi period, the authors became interested in the phenomenon of anti-Semitism. They administered a battery of questionnaires to a group of people who exhibited the most anti-Semitism and to another group that exhibited the least anti-Semitism, and then compared their answers. In this way, they developed the F-scale (Fascism-scale) which enabled them to study the traits of subjects with an authoritarian personality. Some of the main traits were conventionalism, submission to authority, the use stereotypes and prejudices, adherence to traditional values and a tendency to follow the dictates of strong leaders. As these and other characteristics suggest, we see here a picture of people who feel the need to solve problems in monological ways. Moreover, they have a low tolerance of uncertainty and tend to classify others in terms of a good-bad dichotomy: others are judged as "good guy" or "bad guy." The problem with this simplified and mutually exclusive categorization is that it reduces the multiplicity of the position repertoire of the perceived other to one simple strongly evaluative position (e.g. Jews are…; blacks are…; we are…). The result is a set of superficial stereotypes.[2]

Uncertainty in Finances, Science, and Art

The relevance of tolerance of uncertainty is not only of historical significance, but rather it is a highly topical subject as it was emphasized in recent debates around the financial crisis in 2009. In a discussion about the problem of decision making in an extremely turbulent period, one of the commentators referred to the necessity of tolerance of ambiguity:

> Some people have no tolerance of ambiguity and uncertainty and try to draw their analysis to premature conclusions in the name of practicality. Others can handle the impractical holding of mutually contradictory viewpoints, strategies, scenarios, theories and intelligence for much longer, and do not need to close down their thinking prematurely in order to try to exert control today on what is going to prove to be uncontrollable tomorrow and will require a completely different competence, mental set, analysis and approach" (Norman Strauss, *Financial Times,* December 31, 2007).

In my own explorations as a scientist, particularly in my theoretical and methodological work, I have learned to think slowly and to make notes throughout a project (making notes slows down the process of thinking so that new ideas can creep in between the spaces of the words written down). However, when one does this, the receptivity to new thoughts develops in a field of uncertainty as openness to fresh or unusual ideas requires a temporary blocking of automatisms, which by their nature close the range of alternatives. Scientific work, I guess, is unthinkable without a persistent doubt about what "truth" is. Richard P. Feynman, an American physicist who is known for his work in quantum mechanics and who received, jointly with two of his colleagues, the Nobel Prize in physics in 1965 pointed to the relevance of uncertainty tolerance in this way:

> The scientist has a lot of experience with ignorance and doubt and uncertainty, and this experience is of very great importance, I think. When a scientist doesn't know the answer to a problem, he is ignorant. When he has a hunch as to what the result is, he is uncertain. And when he is pretty darned sure of what the result is going to be, he is in some doubt. We have found it of paramount importance that in order to progress we must recognize the ignorance and leave room for doubt. *Scientific knowledge is a body of statements of varying degrees of certainty—some most unsure, some nearly sure, none absolutely certain.*[3]

During my work as a scientist, I was always interested in the relation between science and art. Numerous times I visited my beloved teacher and (later) colleague Karel van de Loo who used to collect drawings from clients suffering from psychosis and had his bookshelves full of books with artistic creations relevant to psychological phenomena. I found out that not only science, but art also profits from the tolerance of uncertainty. Bayles and Orland (2001) phrase it in this way:

> People who need certainty in their lives are less likely to make art that is risky, subversive, complicated, iffy, suggestive or spontaneous. What's really needed is nothing more than a broad sense of what you are looking for, some strategy for how to find it, and an overriding willingness to embrace mistakes and surprises along the way. Simply put, making art is chancy—it doesn't mix well with predictability. Uncertainty is the essential, inevitable and all-pervasive companion to your desire to make art. And tolerance for uncertainty is the prerequisite to succeeding.[4]

In writing this text I myself experience the relevance of uncertainty tolerance very vividly. In my preparation of this book, I collected many notes that I wrote down in my notebooks over the years, and put them in a list. I read and reread them without imposing any structure. I ask myself which of these notes I consider as central and relevant topics to the chapter I have in mind. Then gradually, and sometimes with jumps, a structure emerges. However, I do not entirely complete this structure, but intentionally leave room for new ideas or information, which come in during the process. Then, I discuss the preliminary structure with my wife and colleague Agnieszka, which leads to the addition of new elements or even to a revision of the structure. When I finally start writing, I notice that a text emerges with which I enter into a kind of dialogical relationship. When I add something to the text which does not fit very well, it is as if the text protests, as if disagreeing with the author. Sometimes the text "smiles" at me, while at other times it "grumbles." In the former case, I'm motivated to write the next part, the latter case is enough reason to revise the text, until we, the text and me, are involved in an interchange that moves on fluently. During all those phases, there are many brakes, sometimes of several minutes, sometimes a day or so, during which the process continues, both on the conscious and unconscious level. In all phases described, I explicitly give space for uncertainty tolerance. This tolerance has quite an ambivalent character. As an *ambitious* writer I want to make progress and use my time efficiently so that I finalize at the end of the day a sufficient number of pages. However, as *creative* writer, I'm sharply aware that delay of closure and openness are essential to constructing a text that has sufficient originality. There is an almost permanent tension between the two positions: the first one

---

EXERCISE 5.1
The following questions are intended to explore your experiences of uncertainty and the way you respond to them.

Question 1
Can you remember a situation in your own life, in which you felt uncertain, to a degree that made you feel fearful and insecure? Can you describe this experience here?

_____

_____

_____

Question 2
Do you remember a situation in which you felt some level of uncertainty that you experienced as pleasant or even as fertile? Describe this experience here:

_____

_____

_____

Question 3
When you compare your answers to the questions 1 and 2, what can you learn from it about yourself?

_____

_____

_____

---

wants production while the second one wants innovation and quality. While the first one wants to accelerate the writing process, the second one prefers to slow down. The most satisfying moments are when both cooperate as members of a productive coalition.[5]

FIVE STRATEGIES TO COPE WITH A
HEIGHTENED LEVEL OF UNCERTAINTY[6]

Many times, when I talked with colleagues about the experience of uncertainty, they posed the question of how people *respond* to this experience. How do people react to experience of heightened uncertainty? Here I summarize five strategies used to reduce uncertainty.

1. Uncertainty can be reduced by *diminishing the number and heterogeneity of positions* in the repertoire. We see this often in people who are fully

engaged in a hectic and complex social life, but who at some point decide to retreat to a simple form of life or change their place in order to find peace of mind. Such a decision is often preceded by a gradually increasing feeling of discomfort that may emerge in a period of doubt or uncertainty about the meaning of all the distracting activities in which one is usually involved. Sometimes this change comes as a sudden surprise to people in the environment or even to the person himself. A background position comes to the foreground when the self is in a state of what James (1902/2004) would call "unstable equilibrium": a particular position is "pressing" to become dominant but is not yet strong enough to take the lead, yet pushes enough to increase the tension in the position repertoire. After some time the unstable equilibrium is suddenly resolved, often without strong external causation, by the breakthrough of the position that was already at the background during the period of inner turmoil (see Chapter 4).

2. Uncertainty can be diminished by *giving the lead to one powerful position* that is allowed to dominate the repertoire as a whole. Located in a field of divergent, conflicting or contradictory positions that increase the level of tension in the self, some people transfer responsibility to some external authority, spiritual guru, or strong political or religious leader as a way to reduce the burden of uncertainty when it has reached a high level of negative emotions (see also the authoritarian personality). This reaction can be seen in cases of religious orthodoxy or political fundamentalism as they thrive on simplification and make extensive use of a good-bad dichotomy in the form of moralistic categorizations. This reaction typically originates from a strong hierarchical organization of the repertoire, with one or a few positions at the top dominating all other positions.

However, it should be noted that many people may organize their lives around one or a limited amount of positions of great personal value. A person may find much satisfaction and inspiration in work that provides enough certainty to permit the development of long-term goals. Or somebody may be involved in a stable relationship that offers deep certainty of mutual trust and commitment. Such examples, however, are different from the cases in which people give the exclusive power to only one dominant position in their lives (e.g. religious fundamentalism or political extremism). Whereas the latter case represents monological dominance, the former case allows space for dialogical interchange. That is, in a stable and deep (dialogical) commitment to a person or task, there is space for an open process of question and answer, for agreement and disagreement, and for supporting and critical voices.

3. Uncertainty can be avoided by *sharpening the boundaries* between oneself and the other and between in-group and out-group. This reaction often takes the form of a Manichean set of opposites (e.g. "we" versus "they"). By sharpening the boundaries between in-group and out-group, often associated with placing

one's own group above the other group, an identity is constructed that tends to increase self-esteem and pride ("We are better than others").

Anger is an important emotion that functions as a driving force to sharpen the boundaries between self and other. However, anger is often a secondary emotion that covers another deeper (primary) emotion (Greenberg, 2002). One of the most important primary emotions that underlies anger is anxiety. In discussions that take place in the political arena, many authors refer to "xenophobia" as a signal of feeling threatened by foreigners. Often xeno-phobia manifests itself in the form of anger, resentment, or hatred. However, this anger that emerges from xenophobia functions as a surface expression of a deeper emotion resulting from negatively experienced uncertainty. The boundaries between self and stranger, often going together with the rejection of shadow positions within the self (the stranger inside), are sharpened, par-ticularly when tolerance of uncertainty is reduced.

4. In a paradoxical way, some people try to reduce uncertainty by *increas-ing, instead of diminishing,* the number of positions in the self. At first sight it seems strange to increase the number of positions that has led to a heightened experience of uncertainty in the past. However, one has to recognize that the additional position is expected to give the solace, rest, structure, pleasure, or prospect that other positions lacked. Somebody may hope, for example, that an additional job or hobby gives the "real" satisfaction that earlier activities did not provide; or the relationship with a new partner may give the stabil-ity and warmth that earlier contacts were lacking; or moving to another city, country, or culture is expected to give an adequate answer to existing uncer-tainties. In such cases new or additional positions are expected to provide an anchor in a fleeting or chaotic position repertoire, subjected as it is to an often over-stimulating globalizing environment. However, in contrast to this expectation the inclusion of new positions (of the same kind) to an already crowded repertoire entails the risk of a cacophony of voices.

Above I referred explicitly to positions "of the same kind" because there are, in a very different way, positions that have the power to transform the repertoire as a whole. I have in mind "promoter positions" like an inspiring teacher, the enriching contact with a new friend or partner, a supporting psy-chotherapist or, inside the self, an artistic, religious or spiritual position that has the power to see all existing positions in a new light. Such promoters have the potential to influence the whole organization of the repertoire in such a way that it develops into the direction of a higher level of integration. These positions play a central role in the next (dialogical) strategy.

5. The reaction to uncertainty, central in the present book, is a dialogical one: *going into uncertainty* rather than avoiding it. Entering a dialogue with other individuals and with oneself, opens a range of possibilities that are not

fixed and not predictable at the beginning of the interchange, but remain flexible and susceptible to new input *during* the process itself. In the course of this open-ended and broadly ranged interchange, the initial positions of the participants are enriched, further developed or changed, marginally or radically, by the encounter itself. During the interchange the difference between positions becomes articulated in an accepting atmosphere, or several positions become combined and integrated into new coalitions. New positions or coalitions may emerge as common to the participants and form a basis for creative decision making.

A dialogue as described above takes place, for example, in a meeting in which participants are able to listen to the other *and* themselves in order to provide a workable or creative solution to a question, problem or conflict. It is typical of a deepening talk between friends, colleagues, or even with a stranger, particularly when institutionalized power differences are not too large and participants are able to construct a common dialogical space in which they allow themselves to be influenced by the other participants. It can also happen when you find an answer to a problem in your own mind after you were contemplating on a question that you were not able to answer in a period of futile exploration. In other words, dialogue can be seen as a "travel into uncertainty" with the possibility of uncertainty-reducing *outcomes*. During the entire dialogical process, tolerance of uncertainty is essential to its nature.

For a dialogical response to uncertainty it is crucial to develop a position repertoire that is able to go beyond the all-pervasive good-bad dichotomy. I'm impressed by the fact that, in discussions about the social significance of emotions, compassion is mentioned frequently. From the perspective of Dialogical Self Theory, positions like "I as compassionate" or "I as being close to myself" (including positive *and* negative experiences) have the potential of giving an adequate answer to the pervasive dominance of the good-bad opposition, particularly when this distinction is manifested as a dichotomy with mutually exclusive poles of good *versus* bad.

I'm sharply aware of the fact that the good-bad dimension, often loaded with a strong emotional evaluation, is deeply entrenched in our minds and even functions as a most basic and universal pair of adjectives, as Osgood (1975) has empirically demonstrated in his *Atlas of Affective Meaning*. In social relationships, the good-bad dichotomy, loaded with strongly evaluative emotions, is often used to affirm the self-esteem of individuals and groups (we as "better" than them) and confirm existing (closed) identities. Positions like "I as compassionate," "I as close to myself," or "I as taking into account the emotions of the other," have the potential to allow and consider not only the "good" aspects but also the "bad" aspects of self and other, so that they

EXERCISE 5.2

In this exercise you pose some questions to yourself without doing any effort to answer them. The intention is to hold the uncertainty for some time and notice your experience.

Question 1

Can you pose a question to yourself referring to something significant in your life, without giving any answer? Formulate the question here;

_____

_____

_____

Can you now look at this question for some time, without doing any effort to give an answer? Consider it as a "meditative question." What do you experience when you are doing this?

_____

_____

_____

Question 2

Can you formulate briefly two opinions or two views of life which you experience in your own development as highly contradictory or conflicting and which you cannot easily reconcile with each other? Summarize each of them in a few sentences.

The first one sounds like this:

_____

_____

_____

The second one sounds like this:

_____

_____

_____

Consider the two opinions simultaneously without giving any answer that takes away their contradiction or uncertainty. To what extent can you tolerate the contradiction, conflict and associated uncertainty? Describe your feeling:

_____

_____

_____

receive space for further consideration and response in non-exclusive and non-separating ways. Dialogue *links* "good" and "bad" and has the potential to transcend them instead of separating them.

It would be an error to assume that dialogue implies uncertainty only and excludes any form of certainty. In contrast, there is space for *post-dialogical certainty*. That is a form of certainty which results from going *through* dialogue and emerges on the fertile ground of positional diversity. This happens, for example, when an individual or group, confronted with a complex problem, allows the emergence of a diversity of positions that permit analyzing the problem from different (personal or cultural) perspectives (see also Avruch and Black,1993) Linking these perspectives in the form of consonant and dissonant dialogues leads to a decision that is supported by a broad range of positions in the repertoire and provides the participants with some degree of certainty that is necessary to take an adequate action. This reaction differs from *pre-dialogical certainty,* which attempts to realize certainty *before* engaging in the process of dialogue or even by avoiding it. The pitfall of this form of certainty is making premature decisions and taking actions derived from the cocoon view of one position only.

The five reactions to uncertainty described above can take place in the life of one and the same individual. At times, we want to retreat from the hassles of everyday life or we come temporarily under the spell of a guru who promises us a life free from stress and the burden of uncertainty; or we feel opposed to all the information, advertisements, and people continuously intruding into our daily lives and taking away our peace of mind. Or we feel attracted to a new job or relationship that, we hope, will solve the problems of the past; or we find ourselves engaged in an interchange that is felt to be both confusing and inspiring at the same time. The last experience, in particular, provides an ideal exercise for coping with uncertainty.

COPING WITH UNCERTAINTY IN MY OWN CASE

While writing this text, I was wondering when I had a strong experience of uncertainty. Suddenly, a memory came up from a long time ago. I had written the introduction of my dissertation *Motivatie en Prestatie* (Motivation and Achievement) and showed the result to my promoter Theo Rutten, a much-respected university professor who received some years earlier the position of Minister of Education within the Dutch government. So, he was an admired authority for me. When I was together with him in his office to discuss the text, he looked somewhat skeptically at me from below his bushy eyebrows and then said: "As the reader of your dissertation, when I read this intro, I felt like throwing the book aside," and, matching the action to the words, he threw my text to the corner of the room with a wide gesture, retreating in painful silence for some moment. Then he took a hand-written text from his desk and said: "This is the way to do such a thing"! He had rewritten my own intro, but in a much more fluent and inviting way. When I went home, I felt confusion but also gratitude that he did all that work for me. The initial moment of uncertainty and confusion was later transformed into a valuable learning experience.

However, which of the described strategies was I using in my own life? For sure, I do not feel any affinity with "giving the lead to one powerful position," certainly not to any person or group in my environment. Strongly influenced as I was by the anti-authoritarian climate of the 60s of the past century, I was used to going my own way and to trying to find trust in myself. I also don't feel much value in "sharpening the boundaries between oneself and the other." This only happened when I was involved in conflict which I was not able to solve. I don't feel much connection with "increasing instead of diminishing the number of positions in the self," as I always restricted myself to a limited circle of family members and friends, and in work situations, I needed concentration on one particular subject to which I devoted almost all my attention. But I feel much affinity with diminishing the number and heterogeneity of positions in the repertoire, particularly in periods when I wanted to devote myself to making notes, writing, creative thinking and self-reflection. Therefore, I never became fully engaged in a hectic social life and often had the feeling that, in order to do my work, I became a kind of hermit, but one who preferred to be in close contact with somebody I love.

The last strategy, "going into uncertainty rather than avoiding it" is, as the nature of this book suggests, the most interesting for me. I discovered that life is full or uncertainty, from the smallest moment of going to this or that restaurant, to the broadest and deepest existential issues including, what is the value of my life and what is left of us after death? Only later in my life I developed the "going into" strategy when I learned, gradually, to stay for some time in a situation of uncertainty without responding, more or less automatically, with an immediate solution. Usually, I'm not a persistent doubter at all, as I can make decisions quite quickly and spontaneously, if my feelings and reason both agree. However, when my reason is not sure about my emotional response, I want to stay for some time in uncertainty, because a variety of options are open during that time which gives me the opportunity to walk around with them and consider their pros and cons. When I then make a decision, I do it with a sense of certainty. Also, in cases of internal or external

---

EXERCISE 5.3

Can you formulate two situations in your life, in which it would be productive to tolerate your uncertainty?

First situation:

_____

_____

_____

Second situation:

_____

_____

_____

Question

When you look at your answers to the previous question in this exercise, can you refer to something or somebody (actual or imagined) who helps you to tolerate uncertainty? Give here your answer.

_____

_____

_____

---

conflict, I remain for some time in the "house of uncertainty," avoiding escalation and just observing what happens so that I can find some answers which I think may bring positions together. I'm rather a pigeon but could become a hawk when all other possibilities are exhausted.

WHAT HELPS US TO GO INTO UNCERTAINTY?

One of my arguments in this chapter is that participating in contemporary society, we find ourselves increasingly in fields of uncertainty. However, going into uncertainty is not always attractive, particularly not when it is associated with an increase in negative emotions. Moreover, when moving into uncertainty has the consequence that one or more cherished positions are at stake ("I as convinced about…" or "I as used to…" or "We as believing that…"), it implies some "identity costs." In such cases, one is challenged to open and widen a fixed and closed identity that is based on a strong belief or the superiority of one's self or one's group over that of others. As a consequence, self-esteem, as closely related to one's cherished identity, is temporarily threatened or reduced. What then motivates people to go into uncertainty when it is not clear what compensates their identity costs?

The problem with uncertainty tolerance is that it becomes impossible when uncertainty becomes strongly *intensified* or when it becomes *generalized* over all or most positions of the self or when some *core* positions in the organization of the self are at stake. In such cases, the person is in strong need of some kind of certainty and, as a consequence, is susceptible to one of the strategies that were described before. Paradoxically, going into uncertainty is only possible when there is at some other place in the self some degree of certainty. Some stability is needed in order to cope with instability. Some organization in the self is necessary for productively coping with destabilizing events. My proposal is that uncertainty tolerance can be stimulated and facilitated by the development of promoter positions because these positions have the potential of giving the "certainty of inspiration" or giving a sense of direction.

I see promoter positions as crucial in the social and personal development of the self. Such positions already exist in society at large. We find them in great and inspiring leaders including Abraham Lincoln, Mikhail Gorbatchev, Nelson Mandela, Mahatma Gandhi and pope John Paul II. Such historical giants function as models, even for people *beyond* the cultures from which they originate (therefore, knowledge of the history, also of other cultures and communities, is so important for education). However, we can stay closer to home to find promoter positions in our own environment. When people reflect on their own development, they often refer to a particular teacher who gave them something precious, a thought, insight, memory, or skill that they carry through their whole life as a precious gift. It can also be a good friend, a father, mother, sibling or a colleague, a character in a novel or film or any artistic or spiritual person who contributed something of lasting value to one's personal development. What many of these persons have in common is that they *inspire*. Inspiration, certainly deep and long-term inspiration, is able to function as a compensation for the identity costs as the price for going into uncertainty. When their influence is strong enough, inspiring persons, figures, or characters can be established as promoter positions in the external domain of the dialogical self. They become entrenched as "others-in-the-self" that give us a sense of direction, particularly in situations in which transience, fluidity, unpredicted change and increasing ambiguity are pervasive. This kind of promoter position is very different from what I earlier described as "giving the lead to one powerful position" which induces giving up one's own responsibility. On the contrary, in the case of a promoter position, the self remains *response-able* to a particular social, artistic, ethical, political, or spiritual being. When a sense-giving and integrative promoter position is finding its place in the external domain of the self, it has the possibility to inspire the person to give an *answer* by developing promoter positions in the internal domain of the self (e.g. "I as artistic," "I as the friend of ...," "I as persisting to realize ...," "I as developing my capacities in the service of ...," "I as becoming aware..."). In this way the self is socialized and individualized at the same time.

Certainly, promoter positions in themselves are not to be idolized as "divine devices" that solve all problems in the self. Many people in the past, and some even today, were inspired by figures like Hitler and Stalin or any other dictator, demagogue or seductive teacher. These admirers would probably claim that such figures function as promoters in their lives or in society at large. However, even when such figures are granted a place in the self as sources of inspiration, they fail dramatically when checked on their willingness and capacity to give other individuals, groups or cultures a fair chance to become involved in dialogical relationships. So, promoters need dialogue, with space for *differences*, that is, for all parties involved to give their contributions from their own specific point of view, without silencing their voices.

This dialogical principle, including tolerance for differences and uncertainty, also applies to the self as a society of mind. When I talk with friends and colleagues, they often say that confronted with situations of uncertainty, they "follow their intuition" or they make clear that "they trust their feelings" even when they are not capable of giving explicit arguments pro or contra to any action or decision. In my view, such people use "intuition" and "feeling" as important internal *I*-positions that have a promoter function when faced with situations of high complexity. In other words, in order to avoid the pitfall of following seductive or abusive external promoter positions, you have to develop internal ones that function as guides that help to prevent any blind admiration or uncritical acceptance.

However, here is my counter-voice: intuition and feeling do not necessarily have the last or final word. For sure, they can become relevant voices in the self and they are of vital importance in finding our way in uncertain situations. For the development of the self it is valuable to listen to them as indispensable sources of information. However, there is the risk of falling into another pitfall if we see intuition and feeling as sources of "ultimate personal truth." As Robert Heller said: "Never ignore a gut feeling, but never believe that's enough." The reason is rather simple: they do *not always* lead us into the best direction. They can be erroneous because they typically lead us to take and follow one particular voice (e.g. "I feel I should do that" or "I feel it is better not to do that"). At this point, we arrive at a basic dialogical principle that there is *always another perspective possible*. So, even when you are damned sure that you know something or you should do something, just have a talk with another person whom you trust and who is able to take another perspective. After such a talk your initial perspective may be changed, developed or confirmed. The advantage is that you take a position on a dialogical basis that broadens your initial perspective and makes you more prepared to act in situations of uncertainty.

So, if I'm right in following this line of thought (and feeling), I propose that there is no final truth, neither in the external promoter positions (e.g. inspiring figures in the world) nor in the internal promoter positions (e.g. my intuition, my feeling). Rather, there is an emerging truth in the dialogue with them, that is, certainty is the result of the play of positioning and counter-positioning. This is what I described earlier in this chapter as "post-dialogical certainty."

THE WISDOM OF UNCERTAINTY

In the beginning of this chapter, I depicted the three worlds in which I lived: traditional, modern, and post-modern, three provinces of meaning that I felt sometimes as contradictory and even conflicting in their practices and values. As told, I experienced a significant degree of uncertainty, particularly at the *interfaces* of the three worlds. In my view, contemporary globalizing society brings, sooner or later, everybody to a situation of contradictions and conflicts between traditional, modern, and post-modern values. The reason is that, as participants in a globalizing society, we are meeting the value systems of localities that are, to different degrees and in different combinations, traditional, modern, and post-modern. Our experiences on the interface of these worlds may be prolific in some cases or produce anxiety and insecurity in other cases. In order to find our way in a complex social environment with a low level of predictability, the tolerance of uncertainty and the development of promoter positions in the self are quintessential (for an example of a promoter position in my own life, see Chapter 2)[7].

It is possible, and maybe even necessary, to go one step beyond tolerance of uncertainty. This is what the novelist Milan Kundera (1988) did in his chapter "The Depreciated Legacy of Cervantes." There he proposed that the world of the novel is "the world as ambiguity," in which there is "not a single absolute truth but a welter of contradictory truths," in which the "only certainty" is "the *wisdom of uncertainty*" (pp. 6–7) (see also Seaton, 2007). In my view, ambiguity is not only a feature of the novel, but of life in general. To live means having to face ambiguity and uncertainty. In a life filled with ambiguity from the beginning to the end, we have to go beyond tolerance and move on to wisdom as a creative and practical way of giving dialogical answers.

NOTES

1. For a detailed treatment of the traditional, modern, and post-modern self, see Hermans and Hermans-Konopka (2010, Chapter 2).

2. The theory of the authoritarian personality has been subjected to a diversity of criticisms. Some commentators objected to the psychoanalytic interpretation of personality and to methodological inadequacies of the F-scale. Another criticism is that the theory insinuates that authoritarianism exists only on the right side of the political spectrum. In one study it was found that the anti-authoritarian personality had the same personality characteristics as the authoritarian personality (Kreml, 1977).

3. http://www.internetweekly.org/iwr/scientific_knowledge.html.

4. http://feralknitter.typepad.com/feral_knitter/2009/02/tolerance-for-uncertainty.html, 12 March, 2010.

5. For the notion of coalition, see Hermans and Hermans-Konopka (2010, chapter 3).

6. This section is a revision and elaboration of the same strategies discussed by Hermans and Hermans-Konopka (2010, Chapter 1)

7. The concept of promoter position is discussed in the context of life-long development in an earlier publication (Hermans & Hermans-Konopka, 2010, Chapter 4).

References

Abbey, Emily & Valsiner Jaan (2004). Emergence of meanings through ambivalence [58 paragraphs]. *Forum: Qualitative Social Research* [Online Journal], 6 (1), Art. 23.

Adorno, T. W., Frenkel-Brunswik, E., Levinson, D. J., & Sanford, R. N. (1950). *The authoritarian personality*. New York: Harper and Row.

Angyal, A. (1965). *Neurosis and treatment: A holistic theory*. New York: Wiley.

Avruch, K., and Black, P. W. (1993). Conflict resolution in intercultural settings. In D. J. D. Sandole and H. van der Merwe (Eds.), *Conflict resolution, theory and practice* (pp. 131–45). Manchester University Press.

Bakan, D. (1966). *The duality of human existence*. Chicago: Rand-McNally.

Bakhtin, M. M. (1984). *Problems of Dostoevsky's poetics*. (C. Emerson, Ed. and Trans.) (Original work published 1929 as *Problemy tvorchestva Dostoevskogo* [Problems of Dostoevsky's Art]). Minneapolis: Minnesota University Press.

Barthes, R. (1996). *Image, music, text*. New York: Hill and Wang.

Belzen, J. (2006) Culture and the 'dialogical self': Toward a secular cultural psychology of religion. In J. Straube, D. Weideman, C. Kolbl, and B. Kielke (Eds.), *Pursuit of meaning: Advances in cultural and cross-cultural psychology* (pp. 129–52). London: Transaction Publishers.

Bhatia, S. (2007). *American karma: Race, culture, and identity in the Indian diaspora*. New York: New York University Press.

Bloom, P. (2008). First person plural. *The Atlantic,* November. http://www.theatlantic.com/magazine/archive/2008/11/first-person-plural/7055/.

Broers, A (2007). *Opmaat tot Eeuwigheid–Beschouwingen van Martinus Muskens* [Upbeat to eternity-reflections by Martinus Muskens]. Nijmegen, The Netherlands: Valkhof Pers.

Cahn, B. L., & Polich, J. (2006). Meditation states and traits: EEG, ERP, and neuroimaging studies, *Psychological Bulletin, 132,* 180–211.

Callero, P. L. (2003). The sociology of the self. *Annual Review of Sociology, 29,* 115–133.

Carlson, R. (1971). Where is the person in personality research. *Psychological Bulletin, 7,* 203–219.

Crocker, J., & Park, L. E. (2004). The costly pursuit of self-esteem. *Psychological Bulletin,* 130, 392–414.

Elster, J. (1989). *Nuts and bolts for the social sciences.* Cambridge: Cambridge University Press.

Foulkes, D. (1978). *A grammar of dreams.* Sussex, England: Harvester Press.

Frank, A. W. (2000). Illness and Autobiographical Work: Dialogue as Narrative Destabilization. *Qualitative Sociology, 23,* 135–156.

Fromm, E. (1956). *The art of loving.* New York: Harper & Row.

Gadamer, H.-G. (1989). *Truth and method* (2nd rev. ed; trans. rev. by J. Weinsheimer and D. G. Marshall). New York: Continuum.

Goldstone, J. A. (1993). *Revolution and rebellion in the early modern world.* Berkeley, Cal.: University of California Press.

Greenberg, L. S. (2002). *Emotion-focused therapy: Coaching clients to work through their feelings.* New York: American Psychological Association.

Hermans, H. J. M. (1974). *Waardegebieden en hun Ontwikkeling: Theorie en Methode van Zelfconfrontatie* [Value areas and their development: Theory and Method of Self-Confrontation]. Amsterdam: Swets & Zeitlinger.

———. (1987a). Self as organized system of valuations: Toward a dialogue with the person. *Journal of Counseling Psychology, 34,* 10–19.

———. (1987b). The dream in the process of valuation: A method of interpretation. *Journal of Personality and Social Psychology, 53,* 163–175.

———. (1996). Opposites in a dialogical self: Constructs as characters. *The Journal of Constructivist Psychology, 9,* 1–26.

———. (2001). The construction of a personal position repertoire: Method and practice. *Culture & Psychology, 7,* 323–365.

———. (2006). Moving through three paradigms, yet remaining the same thinker. *Counselling Psychology Quarterly, 19,* 5–25.

Hermans, H. J. M., & Hermans-Jansen, E. (1995). *Self-narratives: The construction of meaning in psychotherapy.* New York: Guilford Press.

Hermans, H. J. M., & Hermans-Konopka, A. (2010). *Dialogical Self Theory: Positioning and Counter-Positioning in a Globalizing Society.* Cambridge, UK: Cambridge University Press.

Hermans, H. J. M., & Hermans-Jansen, E., *Self-Narratives: The Construction of Meaning in Psychotherapy.* New York: Guilford Press.

Hermans, H. J. M., Hermans-Jansen, E., & Van Gilst, W. (1985). *De grondmotieven van het menselijk bestaan* [The basic motives of human existence]. Lisse, The Netherlands: Swets & Zeitlinger.

———. (1991). Self-narrative and collective myth: An analysis of the Narcissus story. *Canadian Journal of Behavioural Science, 2,* 423–440.

Hermans, H. J. M., & Kempen, H. J. G. (1993). *The dialogical self: Meaning as movement.* San Diego: Academic Press.

————. (1998). Moving cultures: The perilous problems of cultural dichotomies in a globalizing society. *American Psychologist, 53*, 1111–1120.

Hermans, H. J. M., Ter Laak, J. J. F., & Maes, P. C. J. M. (1972). Achievement motivation and fear of failure in family and school. *Developmental Psychology, 6,* 520–528.

Hermans-Konopka, A. (2012). The depositioning of the I: emotional coaching in the context of transcendental awareness. In H. J. M. Hermans & T. Gieser, Handbook of Dialogical Self Theory (pp. 423–438). Cambridge, UK: Cambridge University Press.

James, W. (1902/2004). *The varieties of religious experience: A study in human nature* (Gifford lectures on natural religion delivered at Edinburgh, 1901–1902). New York: Barnes & Noble.

Jones, R., & Morioka, M. (2011). Introduction. In R. Jones & M. Morioka (Eds.) *Jungian and dialogical self perspectives* (pp. 1–11). New York: Palgrave/Macmillan.

Kohnstamm. P. (2007). *I am I—Sudden flashes of self-awareness in childhood.* London: Athena Press.

Kreml, W. P. (1977). *The anti-authoritarian personality.* Oxford: Pergamon.

Kundera, M. (1988). *The Art of the Novel* (trans. Linda Asher). London: Faber and Faber.

Leijen, A., & Kullasepp, K. (in press). All roads lead to Rome: Developmental trajectories of student teachers' professional and personal identity development. *Journal of Constructivist Psychology.*

Levin, D. M. (1988). *The opening of vision. Nihilism and the postmodern situation.* New York: Routledge.

Morrison, A. P. (1997). *Shame: The Underside of Narcissism*, The Analytic Presss.

Nir, D. (2011). Voicing inner conflict: From a dialogical to a negotiational self. In: H. J. M. Hermans & T. Gieser (Eds.), *Handbook of Dialogical Self Theory* (pp. 284–300). Cambridge, UK: Cambridge University Press.

Osgood, C. E., May, W. H., & Miron, M. S. (1975). *Cross-cultural universals of affective meaning.* Urbana, IL: University of Illinois Press.

O'Sullivan, R. & De Abreu, G. (2010). Maintaining continuity in a cultural contact zone: Identification strategies in the dialogical self. *Culture & Psychology, 16,* 73–92.

Ribeiro, A. P., & Goncalves, M. M. (2010). Innovation and stability within the dialogical self: The centrality of ambivalence. *Culture & Psychology, 16,* 116–126.

Rowan, J. (2009). *Personification: Using the Dialogical Self in Psychotherapy and Counselling.* London: Routledge.

Sampson, E. (1985). The decentralization of identity: Toward a revised concept of personal and social order. *American Psychologist, 11,* 1203–1211.

Schmoll, J. A. (1978). *August Rodin.* Herrsching am Ammersee, Germany: Schuler Verlag.

Seaton, J. (2007). Lyric poetry, the novel, and revolution: Milan Kundera's *Life is Elsewhere. Humanitas, 20,* 86–95.

Valsiner, J. (2004). *The promoter sign: Developmental transformation within the structure of the dialogical self.* XVIII Biennial Meeting of the ISSBD, Ghent, Belgium, 11–15 July.

Van Geel, R. (2000). *Agency and communion in self-narratives: A psychometric study of the Self-Confrontation Method.* Dissertation, University of Nijmegen, The Netherlands.

Van Geel, R., & De Mey, H. (2003). Self, Other, Positive, and Negative Affect Scales of the Self-Confrontation Method: Factorial structure and unidimensionality. *Personality and Individual Differences, 35,* 1833–1847.

Index